EVERY DOG
NEEDS HOPE

A dog deemed worthless and a charitable scheme that needs her help to continue

EVERYBODY
NEEDS HOPE

A dog deemed worthless and a charitable scheme that needs her help to continue

SOPHIE WELLUM-MAYES

EVERYBODY NEEDS HOPE

Copyright © 2018 Sophie Wellum-Mayes

Publishing Services by Happy Self Publishing
www.happyselfpublishing.com

Year: 2018

All rights reserved. No reproduction, transmission or copy of this publication can be made without the written consent of the author in accordance with the provision of the Copyright Acts. Any person doing so will be liable to civil claims and criminal prosecution.

Disclaimer

This is a fictional biography- As clever as she is, Hope can't actually write, or tell me how she's feeling!! Whilst the story has been based on true events and real people, some parts have been dramatized for reading purposes. Some names and characteristics have been changed, some events have been altered, and some dialogue has been recreated.

Happy Self Publishing.

FOREWORD TO EVERYBODY NEEDS HOPE

It gives me great pleasure to write a Foreword to Sophie…'s book, *Everybody needs Hope*, a delightful account of the life of a lovable but clumsy puppy through the several stages of training under the auspices of *Headway Suffolk* to become a highly dependable service dog. The amount of dedication and patience required of both trainer and dog to achieve this goal is extraordinary, and is little known in the wider community other than to those people working to provide care and help to people with disabilities.

Previously guide dogs were available only to blind people but nowadays the potential of service dogs to improve the quality of life of many people is huge. The service dogs can bring all sorts of benefits: a calming comfort to dementia patients, encouragement to people of all ages suffering from lack of confidence, reassurance and motivation to stroke victims, and additionally as guide dogs, they can care for, lead and protect those whose lives are in danger whether from sudden attacks of illness or malicious elements in the outside world.

Unfortunately, there are few providers of service dogs and of those there are, many charge very high fees and not all are reliable. Sophie.. wants to expand her animal assisted interventions to benefit a wider clientele, including schools, speech therapy, physiotherapy and special needs. Her dogs would then be able to help a wider range of people suffering from many more debilitating conditions than at present, whether physical, mental or psychological. The problem is that funds are running out for the work that she is already doing, and the future is uncertain. It would be terrible if all her hard work were in vain. Her book is a must for dog lovers and anyone interested in the training of dogs, so I am happy whole-heartedly to recommend *Everybody Needs Hope*, and would like to think that the sales of this wonderful book will help Sophie achieve her aim and carry on with her inspiring and valuable work.

Jane Hawking

ACKNOWLEDGMENTS

Wow they weren't joking when they said the acknowledgments can be the hardest bit to write. I mean how do I put in to words how grateful I am to those that have supported, encouraged and read through chapter by chapter.

There are a few names that I would like to say a special thank you to though, as without your continued encouragement; I would never have gotten to this point:

Firstly to my proof readers who took the time out of their own busy schedules to help and encourage me in the beginning stages: Claire Partridge, Leesa Palmer and Jo Gray to name a few.

Also a huge thank you to Phil Owens, who I met when he boarded a dog for us on the scheme. Phil helped take the book to a new level with his expert proof reading and his skills within this industry have been indispensable.

I would also like to thank my colleague on the scheme, Ginette Forbes Smith, for listening to my constant ramblings and for continued support in the day to day running of the scheme.

Lastly I would like to thank the CEO of Headway Suffolk, Helen Fairweather, for initially coming up with the scheme and giving me the opportunity to work in a job I truly love.

PREFACE

When I left university I had an advantage over a lot of my friends; I knew without doubt that I wanted to work with dogs…..I just wasn't sure in what capacity

I have an affinity with dogs and have always preferred their company to that of a human, and without sounding big headed, I knew I could train them. With that in mind, I decided I wanted to train them to help people; but with my student loan hanging over me, a horse to pay for, and a low-paid cashier job, I certainly wasn't in the position to move away to where the jobs were.

So I got a job as a carer: the closest link I could make, and before long I realised I had another skill set.

I worked on the dementia unit and despite long days and hard work, I loved every minute of it. One day, I took my family's boxer dog (Tilly) in to meet the residents, and I literally watched people change in front of my eyes. People that I had never heard speak, reached out and spoke to Tilly; those that never got out of bed, were up and walking down the corridors with me, and it was there and then I knew there was more that dogs could do to help people.

I moved out of home and bought my own dog, and I started to think of ways I could set myself up using dogs as a rehab tool. The road led me to my current job, where I work for a scheme called Brainy Dogs. I won't say too much about the scheme just now, but I will say, it has been a game-changer for not only me, but all those I have worked with.

Along the road, I purchased Hope, and she is helping me reach the goals I set myself back in the care home. She really is a remarkable dog, and all those that meet her comment on how special she is.

However, the scheme is funded, and there is the potential risk that without more money, it will have to stop operating; which is what led me to write this book.

I wanted to make more people aware of what we do, whilst at the same time, create more funds to keep the scheme in operation.

I chose to write the book from my perception of Hope's point of view to give a more meaningful feel to the book. I have tried to include a variety of different angles in the book, from the way in which dogs learn through to the different rewards that dogs can bring to us just by being in their company.

I never set out to be an author; but I hope you will enjoy the story and help support the scheme by recommending to others to purchase and read.

From the bottom of my heart,

Thank you for your support

Sophie Wellum Mayes

MY BEGINNING

My first memory is one of happy remorse; bittersweet some would say. Happy, because that's how it makes me feel when I think back, but remorse that I didn't know what was about to come. For if I did, I would have savoured my time more: laid with my eyes open, watching and resting but not quite asleep, instead of sleeping for most of the day which we all liked to do. I would have taken time to play with my mother more, rather than use her as a walking milk bottle; and I would have enjoyed my brother's constant need to play rather than seeing him as nuisance that needed to be ignored. Now don't get me wrong, for when I say I didn't know what was to come, it was not a bad life that I have led— in fact, the very opposite. But for a young puppy who one day is sleeping safely beside her mother surrounded by her three brothers and a sister, and the next without word or warning is alone in a cold stable with strangers picking her up and examining her like a piece of meat on a butchers stall is a hard experience to look positively on. But I will get back to that day— for now, my first memories....

I was lying in the courtyard that led to the barn where I was born. Inside, the barn was divided into three derelict stables, straw and hay still lined the floor, which protected us from the cold; buckets of water sat in the corner of the largest stable, which provided my mother with water. Next to the big bucket, there was a funny little dish, which we could all drink from as the bucket was too big for us to reach. My mother told me the water container was originally meant for chickens, and as we all came as a great surprise to the farmer, he had to make do with what he had. Outside the barn was a small courtyard, brick walls enclosed the yard, with a big wooden gate leading out to the driveway and the farmhouse. My mother told us that before she came to live here, the barn and courtyard had been used to house the farm horses. But now the farmer had machines to do the hard graft, and so he no longer needed them. Along the brick walls there were still three metal rings that the horses used to be tied to, but now the lead ropes hung abandoned — but for us puppies, they made perfect toys.

My mother told us how the machines worked much more quickly than the horses ever could, meaning the farmer had much more time on his hands. Now in his spare time, he liked to enjoy a bit of shooting — — which is why he had my mother. Many nights, before we snuggled up to sleep, we asked Mother to tell us about her job with the farmer. She told us her job was as a 'flusher' and was the most important one of all; as without her, there would be no pheasants for the farmer to shoot. Her face always lit up when she told us about all the smells of the woods, and how she had to zone in on the scent of the pheasant, and then follow that smell until she would find them hiding — — usually in the deepest of bracken. Then without hurting them at all (that was very important), she would chase them out and encourage them to fly up high out of the woods. Sometimes, if they were very lazy and unwilling to fly, she would nip at their long tail feathers to encourage them. Once the farmer had shot the pheasants down, it was then my father's turn to run as fast as he could, find them, and bring them back without putting a feather out of place with his teeth. I remember so clearly seeing my father trotting back alongside the farmer one day. He glanced in our direction as he came past but quickly turned his attention back to the farmer, who was carrying the proof of my father's good work. My siblings and I all watched in awe of my father from the gateway until he was completely out of sight. My mother told us that our father was the most regal man she had ever met: as gentle as a lamb, but as loyal as they come. She told us how she had fallen in love with him from the moment he first jumped out of the farmers green Land Rover. Initially, they had been kept together in the farmhouse with the farmer and his wife. My mother would spend the mornings cleaning his ears or resting her head across his neck while they dozed in the sun. Then after a hard day's work, they would curl up together soaking up the heat of the fire to ease their worn-out muscles. But one thing had led to another, and before long, my mother was pregnant with us. Initially, the farmer thought my mother was getting a bit heavy and cut down her food. But when he realised she wasn't, he was not happy. He took her by the collar and banished her to the confines of the stables and courtyard that we called home. Occasionally, when we were fast asleep, my father would sneak out on his last toilet duties and lick my mother's nose through the bars of the fence; but his loyalty to the farmer soon had him on his heels and racing back to the farmhouse before he was spotted. My mother hoped that if she was really well behaved, the farmer would allow her back into the farmhouse, but whenever we saw him, he would huff and puff while he threw the food for us over the gate. Every now and again, if she pestered enough, he would place his hand on her head and say, 'you brought this on yourself old gal,' but my mother remained adamant he would forgive her one day.

From that first sighting of my father, we all decided we wanted to grow up to be just like him—in fact, we all became a little bit obsessed——my eldest brother especially. He was a little bit bigger than the rest of us and was by far the most confident. As we grew older, we would make up games and take it in turns to be our father. We would practice our trot along the wall perimeter, putting our nose as high as we could, and try to touch it with our knees as we ran. My brother made sure he always had the first and last go, just so he had one more try than the rest of us. Another favourite game of ours was to retrieve as many leaves as we could without damaging them. We would start off in the stables and then run as fast as we could to the far wall, retrieve a leaf and then gently hold it in our mouths and race back to the stable to place them in piles. Sometimes we would hold a leaf too softly and they would fly out of our mouths, and we would waste time trying to catch it again as the wind took it around the courtyard. Or sometimes we would be too rough with our mouths and put a hole right through the middle for which we had points deducted. My brother always won, but he had slightly longer legs, which I'm sure made all the difference. While I enjoyed the games to start with, as I became slightly older, it was clear that I was never going to be able to keep up with others. My sister was pretty quick, but she couldn't quite get the right hold on the leaves and would either spend most of the time chasing them around or would get so excited she would crush them until they were just confetti. My other brothers were pretty much on par with each other, not quite as fast as the other two, but they sussed out the gentle hold pretty quickly.

However, it was clear that I just wasn't cut out to be like my dad. While all the others looked like mini replicas of him, I had taken on some of my mother's features. When I asked my mother why I looked different to the others, she explained that she and my father were different breeds and therefore looked different from each other. Most parents are of the same breed, so their children come out looking like both of them. However, I was known as a cross breed and so took different aspects of both my parents, and it was just luck of the genes as to how I looked. My mother was a working Cocker Spaniel; she had a lovely curl to her lemon and white coat, she had short legs and beautiful long curly ears. Her tail was docked so it didn't get hurt in the woods, and she was much daintier than a show cocker spaniel. My father was a working Labrador and so was taller than my mother but not as big as a show Labrador, and he had short jet-black hair. My brothers and sister were very lucky as they all looked exactly like my father. However, I had a black coat like my dad but short legs and long ears like my mother. This was why I was so rubbish at the games— —my stumpy little legs couldn't reach very far, and quite often, I would fall over my long ears.

My mother told me that the farmer was so cross with her because children of mixed breed dogs were next to worthless. In fact, many of the farmers' friends had told him to drown us all at birth, but luckily, he hadn't been able to do that. After my mother told me that, I found I liked the farmer a little bit more. Later on in my life, I found out about many of the breeds my mother had told me about— —and I found many cross breeds, too. It turned out that they weren't as worthless as the farmer thought, but he was very old-fashioned in his beliefs. I'm so glad he didn't drown us.

When we were about 8 weeks old, we were all out in the courtyard enjoying the sun completely unaware of what was about what would happen next. By now, we were completely independent of my mother's milk and ate the grown-up food just like her— although our biscuits were somewhat smaller. We would all still try and steal a drink though if she was asleep or we thought we wouldn't get told off.

While I lay bathing in the sunlight, I watched my siblings and thought how grown up we were all starting to look. My oldest brother was playing with a dead blackbird that had flown full pelt into the wall and landed in a heap at the bottom. He put all his leaf practice in to play and picked up the bird as gently as he could. He then proceeded to trot around the courtyard, making sure he looked as fancy as possible when he went past the gate just in case my father was watching. My sister was practising her hold any leaves she could get her mouth on, and she was now only crushing a very few, while my two other brothers were racing each other round and round the courtyard jumping over anything that was in their way — including me!

I must have dozed off watching them all, because the next thing I knew, I was awakened to the sound of the courtyard gate swinging open. I looked up to the see the farmer standing there with a lead hanging in his hand. He stood there for a while looking at us all in turn and then walked over to where my oldest brother was now lying, dead bird laying between his two front paws. On seeing the farmer approach, he quickly jumped to his feet, picked up the bird gently between his jaws, and trotted elegantly over to meet the farmer. I must admit I was jealous of just how much he looked like my father, and I knew that he was going to grow to be a very fine-looking dog indeed.

The farmer let one side of the lead go, so it dropped just in front of my brother's head forming a nylon loop just big enough for his head to fit. Then in one swift movement, the farmer brought the loop over the top of my brother's ears and pulled up so the loop tightened around his neck. This must have shocked my brother as he dropped the bird he had been so proudly holding so it fell between himself and the farmer's feet. He then wriggled back, rearing up on his back legs as he did so, trying to free himself from the lead that was getting tighter and tighter around his neck. He let out a cry of panic, and I saw the fear forming within in his eyes. At this point, my mother ran forward, but the farmer outstretched a hand — signalling for her to stop. The loyalty she held for him stopped her in her tracks, but from where I was now stood, I could hear her whimpering in desperation to help her son.

The farmer, however, seemed to be unfazed by my brother's actions, and he turned on his heels and proceeded to walk back towards to the gate that led to the farmyard beyond. My brother was forced to follow on behind, and every now and again, he would take a step forward in the direction he was going to allow the lead to slacken, which made it more comfortable around his neck. The farmer reached the wooden gate and swung it open, encouraging my brother out as he did so by a whistle and a nod of his head. Beyond the gate, my father sat patiently waiting. On seeing my father, my brother stopped resisting the lead and ran forward in a desperate bid to say a long-awaited hello; but the lead pulled tight around his neck, flipping him back on to the floor.

"You'll learn," I heard the farmer say quietly to my brother.

Then with a nod of his head, he signalled for my father, who obediently trotted out in front of them both and went down the path that led to the old stone farmhouse. My brother met the end of the lead again, but this time copied my father, so he, too, trotted out in front of the farmer. My mother, by this point, had run forward to the gate that held her captive. She placed her nose between the wooden slats and watched as the three proceeded down the path and into the house. She then turned slowly around and walked into one of the cold, damp stables, her tail hanging limply between her legs. My sister playfully picked up a leaf and ran towards my mother in a desperate attempt to cheer her up, but my mother kept walking, eyes down, until she lay alone in the stable; where she remained for the rest of the night.

My siblings and I (confused by what had just happened) spent the remainder of the afternoon watching the front door of the farmhouse, waiting for my brother to reappear and tell us what exciting adventures he had been up to and what our father was really like up close. However, as the sun started to set and the chill picked up in the air, we turned back towards the stable where my remorseful mother lay. One by one, we curled up next to her and snuggled our faces into her long warm coat until we finally fell asleep—we never did see our brother again—or indeed, find out what our father was like.

The next day, we were woken early by the sound of the wooden gate swinging shut. We all stood up in unison and stretched our front legs forward, giving a little yawn. As we did so, my mother never seemed to have time to stretch and was up and out of the stable before we had really found our feet; I think she was still trying her hardest to win the farmer over. We all ran out of the stable, my sister taking the lead now my brother wasn't around, followed by my two other brothers—again on par with each other: and then, me bringing up the rear. As I tried my hardest to keep up, my ears dangled precariously close to my feet. Determined to impress the farmer this morning, I gave an extra spurt—throwing my legs as far forward as I could. But before I knew it, my foot caught the bottom of my ear, pulling my head down towards the ground, my bottom overtook me, and I found myself helplessly rolling head-first towards the farmer. As I stopped, slightly disorientated, I could just make out two burly hands reaching down towards me. The strong grip held me underneath my elbows, and I was lifted high above the ground until I was looking straight into the farmers face. I had never seen him this close before: he had short facial hair that kept his face warmer in the bitter morning wind, some bits longer than others where he had been in a rush to get on with the duties of the farm. His skin was dry, and he had large wrinkles under his eyes—a sign of how the long farm days had taken their toll over the years. His eyes were a deep hazel, and behind the icy exterior, there was unexpected warmth. Poking out from under his tired, tweed cap were strands of wiry grey hair that I had never noticed from the ground. As I studied him, I felt his eyes watching over me in return: he examined my long ears that were just resting on the sides of his hands, and I saw the disappointment in his eyes when he looked at my short stumpy legs that hung helplessly within in his grip.

With a small shake of the head, he whispered, "we'll have to keep you out of sight today littl'un, I'm afraid."

And with that, he carried me away from the others and out of the courtyard. As he took me away, I wondered whether I was going to see my brother again, and I looked up eagerly at where we were headed. But instead of heading down the path where he had proudly trotted along only yesterday, the farmer took a sharp left behind the courtyard perimeter until he stopped at a small shed. He opened the door, and a strong smell of ammonia hit my nose. I wriggled to try and free myself from the smell that was now within my lungs, but the farmer's grip was too strong for my little body. As he placed me down, he laid one hand on my fur, and for the first time, I felt what it was like to be stroked. I felt my body relax as his strong fingers touched me lightly from the top of my head and down across my back. The farmer stood there for a short while with me; apologising for keeping me locked away, and I instantly knew the safety my mother had felt from him until she had been banished because of us. The farmer told me how the visitors were from a very prestigious family, and looking the way I did wouldn't have done him any favours within the farmer's circle. I wasn't sure why the visitors affected me as the farmer often had people come to and from the house, but I remembered my mother telling me how our humans always knew best, and it was our job to simply obey. As the farmer lifted his hand from my fur, I sat back and watched him back out of the doorway, closing the door behind him — leaving me completely encapsulated in darkness.

As my eyes adjusted to the darkness, I started to take in my new surroundings: although, there wasn't much to look at. There were no windows, and the only light was through a small gap where the door had warped over the years, and through a broken plank of wood along the side opposite the doorway. In the far corner piled high to the ceiling and filling up nearly half of the space, was a mound of coal for heating the cold, stone farmhouse. A small rusty lamp hung on a nail by the side of the door, and a metal spade and wooden bucket sat beside the coal. Besides these few thing's the shed was bare and damp, and the smell of ammonia still hung strongly in the air. My keen nose followed the smell to the broken wooden plank where I then tried to peer through the small gap to the world outside. I could see very little, but my instinct told me that the coal shed backed on to the large muck heap where the farmer emptied the manure from the pigsties that still remained active on the farm, and it was a smell I could hardly bear. Rapidly, I backed up from the stench until my bottom hit the coal pile behind, dislodging some loose stones from the top sending them cascading down the pile to where I sat below. At a loss for what to do, I pushed the loose stones to one side and curled up on the cold, damp floor. Despite the hard concrete causing me great discomfort, I resigned myself to the fact that I was here until the farmer came back to let me out; and slowly, I fell asleep.

I dozed on and off for what felt like an eternity before I heard the sound of the door creaking open, and the sunlight flooded into where I lay. The farmer's burly shape filled the small doorway, and before I had time to stand or even stretch, he reached in, picked me up and carried me back towards the courtyard that I called home. I knew a fair few hours had passed since I had left as the sun was now starting to set behind the large pig house. The farmer swung the gate open and placed me down; then, without even a look in my direction, he closed the gate and turned back towards the farmhouse. I looked around for my siblings or mother, but there was no sign of anyone, so I made my way warily into the stables to see if they were there. On entering the stable, I knew something was wrong: my mother once again laid there mournfully with just one brother and my sister by her side. On seeing me, my mother raised her head and wagged her tail limply, then laid her head back down. My sister then proceeded to tell me all about the family that had arrived just after I had left. The family consisted of a young couple and their two children. The couple had gone off with the farmer, while the children—a boy and a younger girl—had spent the day playing in the courtyard. My sister informed me of how the children had not let them rest all day: the boy had chased them around and around, while the girl had picked them up and carried them around like toys. On their parent's return, they had pointed to my absent brother, who, at that moment, was chewing on the toggle hanging from the girl's expensive leather field boots. The man had picked him up and looked him over from top to tail before turning and handing him to the young girl standing excitedly by his side. With that, the man shook the farmer's hand, returned to their car with my brother, and then drove away without a second glance. My mother, once again, had no time to even say goodbye to her child and had gone to mourn in the stable. On finishing the story, my sister, who was exhausted from her eventful day, fell straight to sleep along with my brother. I laid awake for a while wondering where my brother had gone and whether he would be happy. I also couldn't help wondering if the farmer had inadvertently done me a favour by removing me from the courtyard out of sight of the two spoilt children, and slowly I fell asleep.

Over the next few days, we had many more visitors arrive to see us, and for these, I was allowed to stay. Some families had children, some were single men, and some were men and their wives, but the one thing they all had in common was the undeniable fact that they were farmers. Dressed in tweed, quite often with a matching hat and wellingtons or leather boots that reached their knees. Some had a shotgun resting uncapped in the crook of their arm like it was a permanent fixture, and some even put a shot out above the courtyard and watched for our reactions. Of course, none of us even flinched: for the sound of a shotgun, we had heard many a time before from when the farmer would go off with my father and return with two or three pheasants hanging limply by his side.

The visitors would often throw new and exciting toys into the courtyard for us to play with and encourage us to take them back to be thrown again. As per usual, I was always the slowest, and despite trying my hardest, could never reach the toy first. While many of the visitors just seemed to dismiss me and concentrated on playing with my siblings, some consciously pointed and laughed at my efforts.

"That'll never make a gun dog for sure."

And one time, a broad-shouldered older man even said, "fit for nothing that one" and nodded in my direction.

After that, I lost interest in playing with the visitors and would take myself into the quiet of the furthest stable. Sometimes my mother would come to check on me, but more often than not, she remained outside waiting for the moment when she knew another of her children would be taken. Then, sure enough, on the third day of visitors, a couple from the previous day returned with a nylon lead in their hand. They slipped it over my sister's head, picked her up, and placed her in a metal crate on the back seat of their brand-new Range Rover. The couple seemed pleasant, and the lady had a gentle approach, which I think made it easier for my mother.

Then the very next day, my brother was taken away by a young farmer on his own. Once again, my mother went and laid alone in the stable, but this time, I remained in the furthest stable by myself. I was exhausted from all the visitors poking and making fun of me, and for the first time, I wondered if they were right — was I really of no use to anyone?

A few more days went past with visitors still coming to view me, although many didn't stay long — realising I was the only one left. Many commented on how large my ears were and how my short legs were, and how they would be no good for speed. However, some seemed more concerned by my lack of enthusiasm to play and stated: "I was too quiet."

With each visitor that came and left shaking their head, the farmer seemed to become more and more frustrated. I often caught him looking at me with a disappointed look in his eye, and I withdrew into myself even more. I spent more and more time in the furthest stable and only came out into the courtyard when the farmer delivered my food. The farmer had become more and more slack with cleaning out the stables, and by now, the little straw that had lined the floor was totally soiled. Some mornings when I awoke, I felt damp from where the urine and faeces I had been forced to lie on had soaked into my fur.

It must have been a week from when my last brother had left, and the visitors had nearly died off completely when I saw a black car pull up the driveway. I remember it clearly because it was so different from all the other cars that had been before: this was no 4 x 4 or Range Rover, and the lady that stepped out was definitely no farmer. She had black trousers, small pump shoes, and a blue fleece with a logo on the front. I watched as she met the farmer and started walking in my direction. On hearing the farmers voice, my mother appeared by my side. She looked at the approaching lady and whispered softly in my ear "This one's for you – I can feel it" and nudged me gently in the direction of the gate.

The lady opened the gate and stepped in while the impatient farmer remained outside. She knelt down and stretched out a hand towards me. I leant forward and sniffed her, her smell was very different to the farmers that had handled me before. She touched my fur lightly on the back of my head, and I felt the tension ease from my body. She spent a while stroking me, and although I know she had noticed my flaws she made no inclination that she was in any way disappointed. In fact, on stroking my ears I heard her say, "like velvet," and although I had no idea what velvet was, I had a feeling it was a good thing.

She picked me up and gently placed me on my back, all the time talking to me in a calm and quiet voice. While I couldn't understand the words, the tone in which she spoke made me feel comfortable, and I felt no need to try and wriggle free from her hold. As I laid there, I noticed how different she looked from everyone I had seen before. She was very young, with a round face and hair pulled tight behind her head into a bun at the back. Her skin was soft, and she had rosy red cheeks that had not been covered over with makeup. Her touch on my fur was gentle, and as she turned me back and placed me on my feet, I felt an overwhelming urge to crawl back into the safety of her arms.

We sat like that for a while until she slowly rose to her feet and stood and spoke with the farmer. She then turned and walked to where my mother was stood patiently waiting. She removed a small blanket from her bag and rubbed it all over my mother before turning back to pick me up. She then carried me over to her car and placed me inside a crate along with the blanket that now had the familiar smell of my mother.

As I peered out of the window, I saw the farmer whistle and nod towards my mother. Without hesitation, she sprang to his side where he placed a burly hand between the top of her two ears and gave her a little scratch. I watched my mother's posture change as she stretched up into his hand. I then watched her spring down towards the farmhouse where I knew my father and brother would be there to greet her.

As I felt the car start rolling down the drive, I had a sudden realisation that I was likely to never see my mother or the farmhouse again. I felt the grief and panic start rising through my body when the lady on the front seat turned her head and with a loving smile looked at me and said:

"This is the start of a whole new life for you….and from now on, you shall be called Hope."

Unsure of what the future held for me, I snuggled into the blanket with its reassuring smell of my mother, and with the motion of the car, I felt myself slip off to a deep restless sleep.

EVERYBODY NEEDS HOPE

Me at 8 weeks old

NEW HOME
AND NEW FRIENDS

My new home was nothing like the farm and courtyard that I had grown to be so fond of. No longer was I to live outside in a stable with rolling countryside to look upon, but a small house with an enclosed garden surrounded by unfamiliar smells and sounds. On entering the house, the lady — my new human — kept me within the metal cage and placed me upon the floor. I looked around at my new surroundings: there were two doors that led to different rooms, a TV on a stand, pictures of different animals on the wall, and a large comfortable seat on which sat a miserable looking brown terrier cross who was visibly not impressed by my arrival.

That first night was very hard for me. I missed my mum, I missed the farm, and I even missed the farmer with his grunts of acknowledgement. Outside the house, I could hear passing cars and people walking past the window, and I missed the tranquillity that the farm nights would bring. The heat of the house made me feel ill, and the new bed on which I laid made me uncomfortably hot. I tried many ways to drown out the noise and get comfortable, but with every movement I made, the terrier (who I later found out was called Flo) would grumble in annoyance. My new human settled on the couch next to me, which did give me some comfort, but I pined for my mother and would have given anything to go back to where I belonged.

The next day, I was allowed out of the crate, and I quickly learnt that there were many rules to living in a house compared to the courtyard. The main one being I was no longer allowed to toilet wherever I liked, and my human would constantly follow me around and carry me outside whenever I felt the urge to go. Occasionally, I would catch her off-guard, but I soon learnt she did not find this amusing. Over time, I taught my human that if I went to the back door, she could open it and I would take myself outside, relieving her of the need to follow me around.

A couple of days after my arrival, I found my energy levels were still low, and I heard my human speak words of concern for me. I found it hard to hear the noises that I knew were occurring outside, and sometimes, I could see my human was talking to me, but the words were muffled and unclear. She picked me up and carried me to the car, which only a few days ago had taken me from my home, and I wondered if I was going back to see my mother. My tail wagged at the thought, and I felt a small spark rise inside my body. However, we had only been travelling for about five minutes when I felt the car slow and come to rest in a fairly empty car park. My human once again carried me across the stones into the strange looking building. It was a funny smell that hit me as we entered, one of cleanliness but of different animals all at the same time. My human sat on one of the plastic seats that ran along the wall and placed me on her knee. We were alone in the waiting room, and I felt my human's worried touch as she played with my long ears. A man in a coat opened a door next to us and invited us in.

Inside the room, there was a large, black table; fresh with the smell of a cleansing spray. In the corner of the floor stood a large set of scales on which I was placed. The man in the jacket made a note on his paper before summoning for me to be placed on the table. Behind him was a cupboard full of labelled bottles and tablets. In an open drawer laid sealed needles and boxes of sterilised gloves. An old-fashioned computer sat in the corner, and at the top of the screen was my name.

The man spent a long time looking in my ears before he took a bottle from the top of the cupboard behind him. He unscrewed the cap and placed two cold drops into both ears. He then firmly gently massaged the base of my ears, which felt good, and I let the weight of my head drop into his soothing hands. He turned to my human and explained that I had two major ear infections, which were probably caused by my living conditions back at the farm; I thought back to the soiled stable in which I used to lay.

Back at home, my human applied the drops into my ears every day. With each day that passed, I felt a little bit better, and slowly my energy levels started to rise. I thought back to the farm and the cold stable, and while I still missed the safety and comfort of my mother, the longing to return slowly started to disappear.

After I started feeling better, I concentrated on trying to make friends with Flo. However, I soon learnt that she was not only unimpressed by my arrival but had a strong dislike of me. I tried my hardest to change her opinion: I tried to cuddle up to her when I was tired, to share my toys with her, and some days I would even steal my human's socks as a peace offering. Flo, however, was having none of it. She preferred to spend her time alone or curled up on my human's lap. I would have joined them, but the seat they sat on was too high up for my little legs— I would try and try to jump up to them.

After one attempt to get her to play resulted in her snapping at me, my human sat with me and told me all about Flo and why she was so irritable.

For the past two years since she herself was a puppy, Flo had been my human's only dog. They had spent all their time together, and Flo had even been allowed to go to work with her. But a few months earlier, Flo had been diagnosed with a brain condition that caused her to have terrible headaches, and she was in a great deal of pain. As she spoke, I watched the muscles in my human's face tighten and tears started to fall down her face. I felt the sadness emanate from her, and instinctively, I nuzzled in closer, as I had to my mother, in an attempt to alleviate her pain. She told me how Flo had once been active and full of life, and as I looked over to the terrier, now curled up in a tight ball and moving only to eat or toilet, I found this hard to believe. The tears from my human started falling heavier and faster, and I found my fur was getting wetter by the minute. I placed my two front paws, that at this point were big in relation to everything else on my body (apart from my ears that is), on my human's shoulders. I licked away the droplets that were surprisingly salty until I felt her muscles ease and she started to let out a quiet chuckle. Slowly the tears stopped, and she pulled me in close. I felt her nose in my fur as she took long slow breaths, and I stayed there until she was ready to release me. As she eventually pulled away, she looked at me, tears still brimming in her eyes, and in a voice so quiet I could hardly hear she said,

"When Flo goes, I'm going to need you more than you will ever know."

Then she put me down and went and curled up on the seat alongside Flo. Despite my young age, I knew, there and then, that the love between Flo and my human was strong, much stronger than that of my mother and the farmer, and I knew that I wanted to know what it was like to feel such a connection.

From that day on, I had more respect for Flo, and I gave her the space she needed. I played with my toys by myself or with my human, and I curled up alone in my bed. Then one day, something changed. I was sat on my bed destroying a sock I had cleverly removed from the basket without my human noticing when I looked up to see Flo approaching. I dropped the sock and recoiled back in my bed, worried I had done something wrong for which I was now to be told off. Instead, she lowered her head and sniffed me. It was the first time I had been this close to her, and from here, it was hard to believe there was anything wrong. She still had the physique of a healthy dog her age: she had strong leg muscles from when she used to run and play, her coat was shiny, and she had such bright, intelligent eyes. In fact, the only telling signs were a few grey hairs that had appeared on her face that didn't belong on a dog so young.

As she stood over me, I noticed the look of annoyance and mistrust had gone from her eyes, and I wondered if this was the first sign that maybe we could become friends.

After that day, my relationship slowly but surely improved with Flo. She was on new medication that eased her pain, and she became much more amenable to my residence in the home. I watched as she started moving around the house more, she took more interest in the toys that my human had bought for me, and her gait became freer and easier. Over the following days, the look of pain went from behind her eyes; she started to jump up onto the seat that I still couldn't reach, and she would run and skip in the garden when she went out to toilet. I watched my human, in turn, watching Flo, and I could see the fear slowly ease from her face. The dog that she had loved so deeply for two years was returning, and the thought of Flo dying was pushed firmly to the back of her mind. As I sat and watched them play together, for the first time since my arrival, my thoughts changed from happiness to one of dread. As much as I loved to see Flo free from pain and my human joyous at Flo's progress, I couldn't help but wonder what this meant for me. I had been informed early on that I was to take over from Flo, and although I didn't know what this entailed yet, I panicked at the thought of no longer being needed by my human.

I left the two of them playing outside, and I returned to where I now called home. I had gotten used to the heat of being inside, and it was a luxury that I no longer wanted to live without. My bed was comfy, and I slept better here than I ever had in the stable. I had food in my very own bowl, and I no longer had to drink from a chicken feeder but a nice shiny metal bowl that was always kept filled to the brim. I had more toys than I could play with: some made noises, some were soft, while others were hard, and every now and again, I even had a chew to ease my teeth that were now starting to hurt. I knew I would want for nothing in this home, and already I had formed the kind of attachment to my human that my mother had told me about many times. At the thought of no longer being needed here and leaving my human for somewhere new, I found myself very, very sad indeed.

As it turns out, I really needn't have worried, for although Flo was better, her condition still left her with headaches and days where she wanted to do nothing but sleep. It became evident that my human still needed me, and I promised myself, as I had promised my mother, that I would serve my human until the day I could no longer.

It also appeared that it was not only me that realised that there was space in my human's life for both of us, but Flo as well. She started to no longer just accept me but seemed to start enjoying my company. When playing with my toys, she started to join with me. Initially, it started with her taking them and jumping up somewhere I couldn't reach. Or running around the garden and laughing at my attempts to catch her up. My legs, although growing, were still short in relation to my body, and I still found running somewhat awkward.

But some days, she would take pity on me and would let me catch up and grab hold of the toy she had just taken from under my nose. I would try my hardest to take it back, but my body, although as big as hers now, was still weak in comparison. I found my bottom would jump up rather than back with every tug I took, my ears flopping helplessly across my face obscuring my view. Flo seemed to find the most amusement in letting me tug with all my might, then letting go just as I was pulling back. I would shoot backwards with such a force, toy still held firmly in my grasp. And sometimes, I would end up somersaulting backwards or crashing into something behind me. One time, exactly this had happened, and I went toppling into a large vase that sat in the corner of the room. I watched helplessly as the vase overturned and smashed into tiny pieces upon hitting the floor. The noise startled me, and I scooted forward away from the wreckage, tail held firmly between my legs. On hearing all the commotion, my human came down from upstairs. She took one look at the broken vase and shouted at me in anger. I had never seen my human cross before, and I was so angry at myself for it being my fault. As she stood there pointing at the mess, I wanted the ground to swallow me up, and I looked around for Flo for advice—but she was nowhere to be seen. I ended up taking the entire blame for that ordeal, as Flo, I later found out, had taken herself outside so as not to be seen. I had been sent to my bed and was only allowed out once all the mess had been cleared away. I hated the thought that I had made my human cross, and from that day on, I vowed never to play tug in the house again.

After this, I found I had gained more of Flo's respect by taking the blame myself. In fact, there were many occasions after this that I ended up taking the blame for Flo. Usually, this involved our feed bags. Both bags were kept in the walk-in cupboard in the kitchen. Needing different bags due to our ages meant it was a bit of a squeeze, and if they weren't put in just right, the door didn't quite close properly. Flo cottoned on to this quickly, and whenever we were left alone, when the door wasn't shut tight, she would wedge her nose in the gap and wiggle it until it opened freely. She would then go and help herself to the bags of food that sat open on the floor. This sounds quite easy but actually involved a skill that I was far from mastering, for she would stand on her back legs and balance just right so she could get the biscuits without disturbing the bag and make a noise. Out of curiosity and pure nosiness, I would follow her in and pick up any biscuits that made it to the floor when she took a mouthful that was a bit too big. More often than not, she would get away unnoticed, but occasionally, our human would disturb her halfway through. Due to the layout of the house, there were only two rooms downstairs—the kitchen and the lounge, which led out to the hallway and upstairs. Flo would only attempt this operation when our human was either out of the house completely or had gone upstairs. Either way, Flo had a much keener sense of hearing than me and would pick up on signs that our human was going to catch her. She would, therefore, scarper from the scene and curl up in her bed before I even had a chance to realise what was going on. So when our human came into the lounge, she would see Flo curled up, nose tucked under a front leg, pretending to be asleep; and then me—exiting the kitchen cupboard, door wide open, licking my lips from one of the few biscuits I had managed to scavenge. I can see how she would have believed that I was to blame; and you would have thought, at some point, I may have learnt to run whenever Flo quickly disappeared. But truth be told, I really wasn't the brightest spark at that age, and it was how I ended up with the nickname "Dopey". Also, if I had tried, I probably would have ended up falling over my ears and crashing into another prized ornament and gotten myself into more trouble. As it was, I never got too told off, just a disapproving look with the words 'typical Labrador' muttered under her breath.

I learnt within my first few months that mine and Flo's friendship would always be one-sided like this. From playing with me when and if she felt like it down to our sleeping arrangements.

I remember the first time she curled up next to me, I didn't make a big deal out of it, but inside, I thought another barrier in our friendship had been broken. However, the next day when I tried to lay next to her, I was met with a grump and a growl before she stood up and walked herself away and laid somewhere else. Over the years, I worked out it was only when she was cold, or it suited her for any other reason would she bring herself to lie with me.

Originally, I was disheartened when I succumbed to the fact that Flo and I would never truly be the best of friends. But over the years I learnt this was just how she was, and I learnt to love her for it. I knew deep down she cared for me, and I was one of the select few she did.

I think because of her condition, she had learnt to stay away from other dogs in case they jumped on her back and caused her pain. Coupled with the fact that many days she still suffered from headaches, I'm not really surprised she never wanted to play with others. This did, however, lead her to be lonely and miserable. On many occasions, I would try and get her to meet new dogs, but she always told me the same thing

'You go, but I'm quite happy over here by myself.'

Hesitantly, I would leave her and go and play with others: she always seemed happy enough staying with our human, but part of me always felt a disloyalty when I went and had fun without her. Sometimes I would look back and see her watching me. Initially, I thought it was because she was jealous, but I soon learnt she was watching out for me—but I will get to that later. For now, I'll just say that while Flo had her quirks, she was loyal to the few she loved, and I knew that if I really needed her, she would have moved mountain and earth to be there for me.

Apart from Flo, I also made another friend within the first few weeks of my arrival. In fact, she was more than a friend, she was a motherly figure that I grew to respect and trust more than anyone else I have met over the years. Her name was Tilly, and she lived with my human's parents.

I remember the first time I met her as if it was yesterday. I had only been at my new home a couple of weeks, and I hadn't been allowed to see the outside world as I hadn't been vaccinated. So when my human carried me outside to her car, it was the first time I had been able to put pictures to the sounds I had been hearing. The roads were busy with cars, and the air outside smelt strongly of petrol fumes. There were people walking along the street talking and laughing with each other. Over the road, were two children who played on their scooters in the safety of their driveway, their father watching while he mowed the front lawn. There were a few trees that grew on the grass verges alongside the road, which appeared home to a few wild birds; a couple of cats watched them flying to and from the branches while they laid lazily on the fence posts soaking up the morning sun. I didn't have time to take much more in before I was placed safely in the metal crate on the back seat of the car. Flo travelled alone in the boot, for at this stage, she was still very dubious of my presence.

I watched out of the window as we backed out of the driveway and on to the road. I wondered where we were headed and felt worried I was being returned back to the farm. I carried on watching until the passing cars made me feel dizzy, then sat back and listened to the music that played through the speakers by my feet. It wasn't long until I felt the car slow, and I heard Flo moving around in anticipation behind me.

As I was carried to the house, I couldn't help but notice how much bigger it was than ours. There were two large potted plants either side of the newly painted front door, and the front garden was lawn and not shingle like at home. The house was a corner plot, and the front lawn stretched around the side of the house where it met the large garden fence. In front of the garden gate was parking for two cars, and next to the empty driveway, was a double garage. The driveway was immaculate, and not a single weed was growing—a far cry from the mass of green growing between the cracks at ours. Even the wheelie bins were neatly tucked away in a shelter adjacent to the garage.

As we stepped through the door into the recently decorated house beyond, we were greeted immediately by Tilly. I had never in my life seen a dog of such a size, and although curious, I was also rather scared. My human must have noted my anxiety, and she held Tilly by the collar and placed me gently on the floor. I remained where I stood for a moment and tried to take it all in as much as possible. She was larger in height than even my father, and she was solid with muscle. She was a light brown to red in colour with a powerful white chest. She had a big, black muzzle, which was now covered in grey hairs indicating her age. Her jowls hung down past her jaws, white slobber hanging slightly from the edges. I was to learn later that, unlike myself, Tilly was a purebred and was known as a Boxer. I also learnt that her real name, something only pedigrees were given, was in fact, 'Truly Scrumptious,' but everybody referred to her as Tilly.

She had been a surprise for my human when she was still at school. Her breeder had to rehome her due to a marriage breakdown, and so she had been sold for a nominal price. The only thing the breeder had requested was that she kept the name. I know this was a sore point for my human as she always said Tilly was a stupid name for a boxer, but I think it suited her perfectly.

As I stood looking at her from the safety of my human's side, I could see she was much more interested in meeting me than Flo had ever been. In fact, Flo didn't even seem keen on saying hello to Tilly herself and was currently in the following room making herself comfortable on the settee she wasn't really allowed to be on.

Slowly, I crept forward, my tail wagging gingerly between my legs to show my eagerness to meet — despite my anxiety. In return, Tilly lowered her head to my level and let me sniff her muzzle. In spite of her size, she was gentle in her approach, and as we stood there getting acquainted, I felt my apprehension decrease until it had completely vanished. The whole time my human sat there quietly, letting us make friends on our own. Once we had sniffed each other from head to toe, Tilly turned her attention back on my, or should I say our human, as she had been hers for 11 years before I came on the scene. It was as if Tilly had forgotten she was there in her eagerness to meet me, and suddenly the realisation came over her. Despite her age, she still acted like a puppy as she jumped over our human with such force, she knocked her flat onto her back. She then laid her body across her stomach rendering her useless to resist the slobbery kisses she placed all over her face. As I sat and watched the well-rehearsed routine, I noticed how happy my human looked. Her laugh echoed around the room, her cheeks became a rosy red picture of health and happiness, and any tension she had been holding in her body completely vanished.

After a short while, they parted, my human now resembled something like a scarecrow: her hair had been pulled from her bun forming a frizzy mess either side, her jumper hung off one shoulder, and her trousers were covered in short brown hairs. She took the time to quickly undo her hair, run her fingers through it, and pull it back into the bun behind her head. I don't think I had ever seen her hair any other way, and despite her friends always encouraging her to make more effort with it, she always replied with the same response:

'I don't have time.'

And from my short time living with her, I certainly wouldn't have argued with that. She was always up before the sun had risen. Flo and I would be let out for our morning toilet duties while she prepared our breakfast. We would then eat while she disappeared upstairs to get herself ready for her daily tasks. She was then out the door without leaving time to eat. She would pop back frequently throughout the day to let us out and give me my afternoon meal but didn't return properly until well into the evening. At this time, she would feed us our dinner, get herself some food—usually something quick and easy, take Flo for as long a walk as she could manage before finally collapsing on the sofa for a cuddle before bedtime. In those early weeks, I wondered where it was she went throughout the day, but it wasn't until I was a bit older that I was to find out.

Today was different though as it was a weekend — the only two days she would get more free time to do what she wanted, and I was quick to learn that this usually meant doing something with Flo and me, and frequently involved coming over to see Tilly.

Once she had sorted her hair, we all went into the lounge of her parents. Again, it was much bigger than I had been used to at home. There were two large sofas on the two walls either side of the doorway, on which Flo was still curled up, and there was a large comfortable reclining chair in the far corner. Next to the chair were two double patio doors that led out to the garden, in front, laid a comfortable duvet folded in half for Tilly. In the corner on the other side of the doors was a large TV, which was so clean I could see my reflection staring back on the black screen. On the wall opposite the largest sofa was an inbuilt fireplace, a fluffy cream rug laid perfectly positioned in front to lie and soak up the heat from the fire. Positioned around the walls hung many pictures of different faces from young to old. My favourite was a photo of my human lying on her belly tilting a tweed hat with her finger; lying opposite was a younger looking Tilly who seemed to be copying her. There was something about the communication between their eyes that gave insight into a relationship far deeper than anybody would ever understand.

As I stood taking in the new environment, I became aware of Tilly standing next to me; in her mouth hung a long yellow and orange toy. She dangled the toy in front my nose, the rope reminded me of the lead ropes I used to tug back at the courtyard, and instinctively, I took hold. A sudden flashback of the broken vase and my human's scornful face made me remember the promise I made myself about not playing tug in the house, and I let go as quickly as I had taken hold. But Tilly stood there patiently waiting and encouraged me to take hold again, something in her eyes convinced me it was safe to do so: a quick look at my human's carefree face confirmed this, and so I played with Tilly for the first of many times.

Playing with Tilly was very different to Flo. She didn't pull me around or steal my toys; instead, she stood and let me play with the toy in my own way. I was very aware that if she wanted to, she could have flung me across the room with just one movement of her head, but despite this, I knew without a doubt, I was safe with her. She played with me until I was so tired I could hardly stand, and then when she knew I had had enough, she laid down on the rug in front of the fire. I curled up beside her and fell fast asleep to the sound of her deep relaxed breaths, knowing there and then that I wanted to be just like her when I grew up.

After I awoke, I laid with Tilly and listened to many of the adventures her and my human had taken together. She told me of the time when she herself was a puppy, not much older than I was now, and how she would have drowned if it wasn't for my human jumping in to rescue her. They had been out for a walk in the countryside near where they used to live when my human still lived with her parents. Tilly had been let off the lead for the first time, and her curiosity had gotten the better of her. They had been walking alongside a fast-flowing stream, the path a few metres higher than the ravine in which the river flowed. Tilly had wandered over the edge to peer down at the river, and a stick caught in the reeds caught her attention. She moved closer to the edge in an attempt to reach down and grab it; she heard our human call her back, but being young and naïve, she ignored the warning tone in her voice. She stepped on a clump of grass overhanging the verge, which gave way under her weight, and she fell head-first into the gushing water below. She tried with all her might to keep her head above the water, but her clumsy, weak legs were useless against the current, and she was forced back under before she had a chance to catch her breath. But before she knew it, our human had jumped in after her and pulled her out from the peril of the water. Back on dry land, she looked up at our human who was now standing in dripping wet clothes, her valuables dumped in a pile on the verge at their feet, and she knew that with her, she was safe.

At this point in the story, Tilly turned to look at me, her face had changed, and a sense of seriousness crossed her eyes,

'There will be times when we can be silly with our human, when we can run and play. But there will be times when we must listen. Learn to hear the different tones she speaks; for most will be happy but some will be angry, some will warn of danger, but the most important is a tone of sadness. Our human will always be fair to us: she will feed us, keep us warm and keep us safe. She will play with us, and you will never want for anything while you are in her care. But there will be times when she will need you but will not ask. You must learn to sense these times, for we owe her this one thing: it is the only way in which we can repay for everything she offers us. In these times, you must be there, no matter how you are feeling, the loyalty to her must come first. If you forget everything else I have told you, promise me you will remember this?'

Although the words confused me, I nodded in agreement. Then, with a look of great sadness, she turned her gaze to our human who was sitting comfortably on the sofa with Flo by her side.

'I won't be here forever to uphold that duty, and I must trust in you to keep it up.'

And with a low groan, she lowered her head to the floor, her gaze still firmly on our human.

'I promise,' I whispered, and snuggled my body that little bit closer to her ageing body.

Me, Tilly and a very grumpy Flo

THE OUTSIDE WORLD

When I was about 12 weeks old, everything started to change. The first sign came in the form of a red nylon collar; a small silver tag hanging from a small metal loop. My human came home one evening with it proudly hanging from her hand. In the other hand, she held a matching red lead. On seeing them, I had flashbacks of the visitors that had taken my brother and sister, despite it being only a few weeks ago, to me, it felt a lifetime ago, and I was desperate not to go back. As my human knelt down and placed the collar around my neck, I felt myself recoiling back from the sudden restraint. Panic rose up through my body at the thought of being taken away from the friends and humans I had learnt to love. My human remained calm and patient, and once the collar was secured and fitted, she sat and stroked my head. I felt myself ease under her touch until I had forgotten all about the farm and going back. Once my human left me, I suddenly became aware of the irritation around my neck. The tag jingled with every step I took, and the collar rubbed my hair around my neck. I tried everything I could think of to remove it: firstly, I tried scratching it off with a hind foot, but I kept losing my balance and falling over backwards—scared I would knock into something and break it, I moved on to a different technique. I tried turning my head, so I could grab it with my mouth, but every attempt was just out of my reach. My ears would flap and hit me in the face, which soon got on my nerves, so I moved on to yet another method. Rubbing my body up and down the sofa, I tried my hardest to push it up over my head. A couple of times, I felt it move, but no matter how hard I tried, it just wouldn't go over my ears. As I sat there feeling defeated, Flo walked over to me and looked at the new article around my neck. She read my name aloud and recited the number for people to ring if I was ever to become lost. She explained to me that as annoying as it was, the collar and tag meant I now truly belonged, then with a sly smile, she turned her back and went back to lay on the sofa. I walked out to the hallway where a full-length mirror hung on the wall. As I looked at my reflection, I was no longer drawn to my ears or my short legs, but at the red around my neck and the tag that glistened in the light—a symbol of belonging and of times to come. I felt proud and grown up, and from that moment on, I never wanted to take it off.

The next day, I was placed in the car alone. It was strange not going with Flo, and I couldn't help but wonder where we were going. As we drove along, I was aware of the route we were taking, and sure enough, we soon pulled up in the carpark I had been to only a few weeks before. However, this time, when we entered, we were not alone. Opposite us sat a lady with a very old greyhound. He wore a blue jacket over his thin skin to keep him warm due to his lack of fat. His face was grey, and he had a large wart protruding from under his left eye. He had a sad look about him, and when his human stood up and started walking to one of the open doors, he remained steadfast, refusing to move. His body was trembling in fear until a large man, different to the man I saw before, in a white jacket came and gently picked him up and carried him in behind his human.

As a door down the corridor opened, a lady in a blue shirt appeared carrying a young kitten against her chest. I peered through the gap into the room behind. The room was lined with cages, some were empty, but many were occupied with different animals of different shapes and sizes. In the closest one, I could see a large black and white cat lying motionless. Taped to its front leg was a tube that ran out through the gaps in the metal cage and hooked up to a machine; hanging from the side was a bag filled with clear fluid. On the cat's back leg was an artificial blue stocking made from bandage, thick cotton wool protruded from the top. Before I could see anymore, the lady with the kitten returned to the room, closing the door behind her. I felt a shiver go up my spine, and my fur stood up on end as an uncontrollable shake took over my body. I snuggled back into the comfort of my human's chest to which she calmly placed a hand upon my head and once again eased away my anxiety.

Not much time had passed before the door to which the greyhound had disappeared opened, and the owner appeared. I held my breath scared for the outcome of the dog, and I wondered if he knew what happened to the poor animals out the back. But just behind the lady, I saw the grey muzzle appear, and the old, frail body plodded along behind her. The cyst was no longer on his face, but a small red area with a drop of blood was in its place. Confused as to what this place was or why my human had brought me here, I once again shuddered at the fear of what was to come. And before I knew it, the man in the white jacket had appeared and beckoned for me and my human to enter.

I saw the man take two gloves from the drawer and place them on his hands before turning to face me. His burly hands reminded me of the farmer's, and I held my breath as he placed them on my head. I sat as still as I could while he looked inside my ears, then in my mouth and at my eyes. But when he took a long, cold, thin instrument and placed it in my bottom, I drew the line. I ran forward and wriggled to try and free myself, but he was too strong and held me still. Even my human appeared to be on his side, and despite saying calming words, she kept me within his grasp.

He then turned back towards the cupboard, pulled a needle from the drawer and a small bottle from the right-hand side of the top shelf. I watched him insert the needle into the bottle and draw up some of the fluid contained within. He then walked to me with the needle behind his back as if I wouldn't see it. He took my scruff within his grip and swiftly inserted the needle through my fur and skin. The pain shot through my body like an arrow, and I couldn't help but cry out in pain. My human raised me to her chest and eased my pain with her soothing words. She then nodded in the man's direction and thanked him before turning and carrying me back to the car.

The next day, I felt woozy and was unsure what the man had done to me, but my human had assured me it was for the best and would lead to many adventures. I thought back to the stories Tilly had told me, and I decided not to question it anymore; and I was right to do so, for the very next day, I got my first taste of the outside world.

It was early in the morning, after we had been fed and let out, and my human was dressed in her casual clothes. She attached the red lead to my collar, which I had now learnt to forget about, and opened the front door. This time, instead of picking me up and carrying me, she encouraged me to take my first steps outside. The tarmac was colder than I expected, and from down here, my nose detected many curious smells. I let my nose lead the way away from the safety of the front door and along the street I had been driven so many times before. I could detect the cats that were often spotted sunning themselves on the fence, the dogs I'd heard walking past the window, the children that passed the house daily on their way to school, and every now and again, the faint smell of a piece of food that had been dropped by children in their strollers. My nose was in overdrive, and I darted from left to right across the path trying to make sense of this new world that was now available. I stopped to smell the flowers that were growing on the grass verges below the trees, where I knew birds would be hiding from the neighbouring cats. I stopped to watch the children playing in their driveways, and I watched in admiration the adult dogs that bounded effortlessly after balls in the park beside the shops. My human seemed happy to let me explore, and she followed on at the other end of the lead. It was only when we had been out for a while and my legs were getting tired that she intervened and encouraged me to turn and walk back the way we had just come

'That will do for today, Hope, there will be plenty more times to explore.'

Upset to be turning home when there was still so much to see and smell, I refused to turn around. I felt the pressure on my neck as my human encouraged me to turn back, but still, I refused to move. In the park, I could still see the older dogs playing, and I tried to show my human my enthusiasm to go join. I strained at the leash, the pressure getting more intense the more I pulled, but she remained steadfast. She stood there patiently while I had my tantrum, and then when I realised that this was something I wasn't going to win, I turned and followed her back towards the house. After a couple of steps, I forgot I was sulking, and I ran past her legs until I was in front, being held back by the lead and collar that was still firmly in place around my neck. I thought it would be boring on the way home, that I had smelt all there was to smell—but I was wrong. The wind was blowing in my face this way, and I felt my ears blowing awkwardly out behind me. With it, the wind carried smells from further afield: chicken that was probably being roasted for someone's Sunday lunch, the cows that were kept in the fields just a few minutes' drive away, and many more that I had yet to learn.

After that, I went outside every day, sometimes only once but many days at least twice. I learnt so much in the weeks that followed, mostly good, but some bad. I learnt that people come in all shapes and sizes: short to tall, skinny to large, noisy to quiet, and most importantly, some like to say hello, but some don't appreciate muddy paw prints on their newly pressed cream trousers. I saw people in trainers, people in boots, men in hats, and women in scarves. Children crying, children laughing, parents shouting, and parents running after screaming children who didn't want to leave the park. I met all sorts of dogs, too: cross breeds and mongrels, and many pure breeds like Tilly, too. I met dogs smaller than me, taller than me, skinnier than me, and fatter than me. Some were hairy, some were hairless, some had haircuts, and some were in need of haircuts. Some were friendly, some were overly friendly, some didn't want to know me, and some had to remain on leads as they weren't at all friendly.

Most of these things I found out quite easily, just by being outside: it was impossible not to notice. My human also made a big effort to get me to see as many things as possible, as it was something called socialisation. This was great, as it meant not only did I walk around the pathways near our house, but we also went out in the car to places other than the vets and Tilly's.

One place I remember well was going to the beach. I remember driving up the road, and the air changing as we approached. There was a funny smell, kind of like fish and salt and rotten seaweed all rolled into one. As the car stopped, I looked out of the window. There were more people than I could ever have imagined. There were couples holding hands, children eating ice cream, adults eating chips out of newspaper, and wet dogs bringing back balls that had been thrown into the sea. My human had brought me alone to the sea, despite Flo's desperate attempts to join. She told me how she had loved the beach, not really one for swimming as such, but she loved running through the shallows dodging the bigger waves that would try to catch her off-guard. However, since her diagnosis, she had been banned from going as the stones played havoc with her back, and she would end up crippled for days after. Even though she knew it was for the best, the look of disdain when we left was something that I could hardly bear.

As I stepped out of the car on to the concrete path that ran parallel to the beach, I was instantly hit by the powerful breeze that came off the sea. It blew particles of sand and grit in my eyes forcing me to turn my back as an escape. As I turned around, I was amazed at the bright lights that paved the street over the road. Above most of the doors read the word 'amusements.' Each one was filled with activity, and the laughter from within could be heard clearly outside. Lining the pavement were machines filled with different teddies; by some stood children tugging at their parents' sleeves pleading for another turn, none of the parents seemed too keen to spend any more money and tried distracting them with something else. Then there were mini rides for children that seemed to run on the spot: some children appeared scared, some bored, but those that enjoyed it wanted to go again and again. The noise and the lights captivated me, and it wasn't until I felt my human tug gently on my lead that I snapped out of it and turned my attention back to the beach and the sea beyond.

We started off along the promenade as the beach itself was so busy and a little off-putting to me. I said hello to the ladies that were sitting on the benches reminiscing about the days when they were younger. Some were drinking tea from polystyrene cups, while others had been more prepared and brought thermos flasks from back home.

A little further along, the promenade quietened down and fewer people occupied the beach. My human carried me down the big concrete steps that led from the path on to the shingle below. I felt my feet sink through the stones pulling my little legs down until I was barely above them. Each step I took was a great deal of effort, and I wondered what all the excitement was about—I didn't like this one bit. However, as we neared the sea, the stones became shallower and easier to walk through, and my body started to shake in excitement of the approaching waves.

The ground in front of the sea changed from shingle to sand, and there I stood, transfixed by the motion of the waves; the attack of the approach and the tranquillity of the retreat: a small white layer of foam left as a reminder. My human seemed to sense my curiosity, and she bent forward and carefully unclipped my lead from my collar. Despite the potential freedom, I had no need to run away from my human, in fact, it was with her, I felt safest—and I think she knew it. But now, I no longer had the lead holding me back, I was free to explore, and I made my way closer to the sea. As I followed a wave back out, the sand became wet under my feet, and I felt myself sink slightly. I looked down to check I wasn't sinking too much; relieved that I wasn't, I looked back up to see a fresh wave fast approaching. Suddenly scared, I ran back as fast as I could, my big, clumsy paws were still too big in relation to my legs, and I found myself struggling to keep upright as they all became entangled in a giant mess. I found myself falling backwards on to the wet sand, and out of the corner of my eye, I could see a wave fast approaching. I tried to right myself, but it was no good, the wave made its attack, and before I could take a breath, I was completely covered in the watery blanket. Within seconds, it retreated, and I managed to right myself, spluttering with the disgusting salty taste that had made its way in my mouth and up my nose. As I tried to shake the water from my coat, I could hear my human laughing—I couldn't see what was so funny and hastily made my way away from the water's edge. After that, despite great effort from my human, I refused to go anywhere near the sea. My human even removed her shoes and socks, rolled up her trousers, and paddled in the shallows, calling my name as she did so. Despite the wish to forget my fear and join her, I couldn't bring myself to. Instead, I remained in the safety of the dry sand and barked several warnings to urge her to come out. After what felt like an eternity, she seemed to see sense and came out and joined me on the sand. As she sat down to dry her feet, I became overrun with excitement that she was back with me, and I gave her lots of kisses, so she knew how grateful I was that she had listened to me. However, despite my anxiety, she insisted on laughing and was adamant that I would learn to love the beach—I wasn't too sure she was right.

A few weeks later, despite my protest, we did indeed return to the beach; but this time with Tilly in tow. As we walked down to the sea, I found myself feeling much more confident with her by my side. She strolled into the breakwater like it wasn't even there, then turned to look at me standing hesitantly in the sand. She barked three times and then proceeded to jump her front legs up and down causing the water to splash impressively by her side. Watching her have so much fun made me completely forget the last time I was there, and slowly, I made my way until I was safely by her side. For the remainder of the day, Tilly showed me all the great things we could do at the beach: we picked seaweed from the shore and chased each other up and down in the shallows, we dug holes in the wet sand, and we laid soaking up the sun when we became tired. Tilly also showed me the delights of running as far into the water as possible before her feet could no longer touch the bottom, then turning and running full pelt at our human, jumping and placing her wet body on her dry clothes and listening to her squealing and laughing as a result. She would also pick unsuspecting passers-by to walk up behind and shake the water from her body at them, then run away before they had a chance to scold her.

After that day, I found myself becoming excited at just the thought of going to the beach. I did, however, make sure I played it down when I returned home to Flo just how much fun I had had. Deep down, I knew all she had to do was look at the sand or smell the salt that still cased my fur to know I had had fun, but I think she appreciated that I kept it quiet.

In those weeks after my vaccination, I also learnt where it was my human went to during the day, and why she returned with a funny smell on her boots.

I sat and watched as she put them on, along with her skin-tight trousers and red waterproof jacket; fleece-lined to keep her warm. I had watched the routine many times and was aware I never got to go. Since she had been feeling better, Flo had sometimes been allowed to join her, and she always came back tired but content. I tried to ask her where it was she went, but she always smiled and said, "you will have to wait and see — but it will be worth the wait." Then she would jump on the sofa, curl herself up, tuck her nose under her leg, and fall fast asleep.

So this time, as I watched my human zip up her coat, I was surprised to see her reach for my lead, which hung by the front door, then with a nod of her head, she signalled for me to come too. She placed me in the car, and for the whole journey, I reached up so I could see out of the window at where we were headed. After about five minutes, the car slowed, and we turned in between two large metal gates, in front of each was a small brown statue of a horse's head, which kept them pinned back, enabling us to pass. We drove past a large house on the left-hand side and then a few wooden stables. On the right-hand side was a large field where two horses stood side by side grazing and soaking up the sun. As we turned the corner past the last stable, the yard opened up, and there was activity everywhere: children on bikes, dogs running loose, chickens running from the dogs, and adults stood talking with mugs of tea in their hands. Before my human even had time to get me out of the car, I was greeted by three of the many dogs running around. They were nearly all Jack Russells apart from two larger Alsatians. I later found out the first to meet me were called Floyd, Jude, and Jamie who were mother, father, and son. In fact, all the Terriers were related to each other and they had very strong family ties: Jude and Floyd were the parents to not only Jamie but Mitzi and Brodie the twins too. Then there was Heston, who was Floyd's brother and, therefore, uncle to the others. It took me a while to work out who was who, as apart from the twins who were white and brown, all the others were black and tan and looked very similar to each other. The two Alsatians were fierce looking and spent their time parading around the yard looking out for anyone they didn't recognise: it took me a long time to summon up the courage to meet them.

As the Jack Russells came over to say hello, I was a little bit taken aback and found myself hiding behind my human's legs. Flo, as usual, had no time for socialising and had already strolled past them all and was currently drinking tea from one of the adult's mugs that had been left unattended. Barely seconds into the greetings, the dogs suddenly scattered as the children, who had heard of my arrival came running over to meet me. There were lots of oohs and aahs in my direction and many statements of 'look at her ears' followed by lots of children's laughter. I was passed from one to the other and prodded and pulled about, and not only by the children but also the adults who had come over to finally meet me. Apparently, they had heard all about me and were desperate to have a 'puppy cuddle.' While part of me wanted to jump down away from the grubby fingers, I remembered my mother's words about remaining graceful and obedient to our human's wishes, and so I stayed still until my human finally rescued me. She placed me gently on the floor and then took me to explore the yard that later would be a daily part of my life.

There was so much to explore that it became clear why Flo loved coming up here so much. To the left of the cars, we went past an outbuilding that was lined with feed bins and bags spilling over with grasses and chaffs, which I presumed fed the horses. A cat sat watching me from the safety of a ceiling beam: its eyes on full alert for any mice or rodents that tried to have a free meal from one of the bins.

Beyond the feed room, the yard opened up into an enclosed square. It reminded me of the courtyard back at the farm, and the smell brought back familiar memories. Along the short sides were walls with metal rings to tie the horses to. A couple of lead ropes and halters hung down from where the horses had been tied and ridden out. Along both the long sides were rows of stables, many were empty, but a couple had sleepy horses' heads appearing over the door, their faces soaking up the sun as they dozed peacefully.

My human walked over to one of the empty stables and swung back the wooden door. Inside, the floor was covered with a thick bed of fresh straw, a few poos were deposited in neat piles, the steam still rising from one. A bucket of water stood half full in the corner and a small pile of uneaten hay in the other. Once in the quiet of the stable, my human reached down and unclipped my lead leaving me free to explore the new environment. As my human took the wheelbarrow that had been neatly leant against the wall next to the door, Flo appeared from around the corner and stood next to me. She took one look at the fresh straw, and before I knew it, dived head-first into it, appearing only when she reached the wall at the back. She encouraged me to join her, and before long, we were chasing each other around and around through the straw, dodging the poos as we went. I had never had so much fun, and I had certainly never seen this side of Flo before. It was like she was a puppy again, and for a while, she seemed to forget about her pain and appeared truly happy. I still wasn't very agile on my legs, and although I was generally more co-ordinated, the straw made it hard, and I kept falling face first into the straw. The dust accumulated up my nose, and before long, all play had ceased while I had a massive sneezing fit in the middle of the stable.

My human had spent the whole time watching us and laughing, occasionally throwing handfuls of straw into the air for us to catch. But now that we had stopped, she looked to her daily jobs of getting the stable ready for another night. At this point, Flo became bored and found a stick to chew outside the stable, but for me, this was all new, and I was intrigued to find out more, so I sat and watched my human as she continued on. To start with, she fished the poo out from the straw with a large metal pitchfork and shook it free into the wheelbarrow, returning the clean straw back to the bed. After all the poo from the top of the bed had been discarded, my nose detected one that had become hidden when Flo and I had been playing. In my eagerness to help, I ran forward to show my human where it was; but she had already seen it, and in the time it took me to get to it, she was already there with the end of the pitchfork. I realised too late that she didn't need me, and I ended up running into the side of the metal prong as it was lifting the poo from under the straw. The force of the collision knocked the fork sideways, and the nuggets of poo separated and spilt back into the bed, making my human cry out in annoyance as they did so. As she bent down to pick up the nuggets one by one, I once again tried to help her; but as I picked up a nugget, it broke in my mouth, creating bits that were now too small to pick up. A stern look came across her face, and she pointed to the stable door:

'OUT,' she cried, before turning back to pick up the remaining nuggets. I slunk out of the stable, eating the half of poo that remained in my mouth. While it tasted good, I couldn't enjoy it knowing that my human was angry at me. When she appeared from the stable and saw me sitting forlornly on the concrete outside, she bent down to stroke my head. Eagerly, I jumped up to kiss her to show how sorry I was, but my breath was a bit smelly from the poo, and I only made matters worse. At this point, Flo had finished her stick and came over to where I was now sat—worrying about doing anything else wrong.

'She'll soon forgive you,' she said, 'that's the benefit of being a dog,' and with that, she laughed and trotted off after my human who was now pushing the full wheelbarrow towards a large muck heap beside the feed store we had passed earlier. Worried I would be forgotten about, I ran to catch them up, and sure enough, Flo was right—my human turned around and gave me a great big smile when she saw me following on obediently behind.

After the wheelbarrow had been emptied and returned, we walked back past the adults, who were drinking yet another cup of tea, and into a big barn that was full to the ceiling with bales of straw and hay. While my human filled a large net until it was stuffed full of hay, Flo showed me how to check between the bales for signs of any mice that the cats hadn't managed to find. She told me how one time she caught a rat that was twice as long as herself and had been just millimetres from biting her jugular—I'm not sure just how truthful it was, but she seemed very proud of herself, so I just nodded in respect.

As we left the barn, the chickens that I had seen earlier were now pecking leftover corn from outside their coop. They were bigger up close than I had first thought, and the cockerel was actually taller than me in height. My curiosity once again took over, and I ran over to say hello. As I ran forward, Flo barked a warning to me, but it was too late: the chickens saw my approach as a threat and scarpered in different directions. They flapped their wings and scooted away as fast as they could; half running, half flying just above the ground. They squawked warnings to each other as they went, which created an almighty row. I followed in hot pursuit in a desperate attempt to show them I meant them no harm, but it was no good. Before I knew it, the cockerel had decided it necessary to protect the hens, and he turned and ran towards me, beating his wings hard against his side making him look tremendously scary. I stopped in my tracks, suddenly aware that his approach was not meant in kindness. I tried to turn away, but it was too late, he was already within inches of my face, and he jumped forwards, legs outstretched in front. I could see his large spurs on the side of his legs aimed in my direction, and it was all I could do to close my eyes and crouch to floor, his spurs narrowly missing the top of my head. As I stood back up and attempted to run back to the safety of my human, he attacked again, this time his legs hit the top of my tail, and I let out a large cry of surprise and panic. Luckily, as I ran forward, I managed to outrun his third attack, and he remained where he had landed. I kept running until I was safely behind my human's legs, and it wasn't until I stopped and peered out from behind that I realised I was still crying in shock. The cockerel stood for a while, his feathers puffed out sideways making him now look even larger than he was before. When he realised that I meant no harm, he returned to his hens who were now huddled a few feet away watching the commotion from a safe distance. As I finally calmed down enough, my human led me past the chickens that had now completely forgotten about what had just happened and returned to eating their corn. I kept my head down and muttered my apologies as I went, not wanting to give them any reason to come at me again.

After this, we continued around the track, which I found out made a complete circuit until it reached back to the main car park. In the middle of the track stood two rows of kennels looking in at an enclosed lawn in the middle. Occupying the kennels were lots of dogs; all of different shapes, breeds, and sizes. Flo told me they were all here for different reasons, mostly because their humans had gone on holiday, but some because they had been left and were looking for new homes. In the middle of the lawn an elderly dachshund stretched his legs in his break from the kennel, Flo told me how she had heard from Jude that his human had died, and he was to stay here until they could find him a new one. I instantly felt sorry for the dog hobbling around on his arthritic legs, and I hoped someone would take him soon. I remember wondering if my human would take him home, I wouldn't have minded sharing my bed, and I think even Flo felt a bit sorry for him. As he headed back into his kennel to rest, we continued off around the track. On the other side from the kennels, the land opened up and stretched back to the tree-line in the distance. The land was divided by wooden fence rails, and in each section stood one or two horses grazing or dozing in the sun. As we walked along the fence-line, one horse raised its head from where it stood grazing and called to my human. Flo informed me that her name was Cuba and was my human's pride and joy. I couldn't really see her from where we stood, but I looked forward to meeting her properly and wondered if we, too, would become friends.

We then slowly made our way back to the car, my legs tired from all the exploring. In fact, by the time we reached the car and my human had placed me in, I was nearly asleep. On the journey home, I dreamt about all the new and exciting things that I was likely to do up at the yard—but maybe next time, I'd give the chickens a wider berth.

My first walk

STARTING WORK

When I was four months old, I was no longer left at home during the day. Instead, I began going to work with my human. I remember the first day as if it was yesterday: it started off with my human placing a brand-new, purple and white collar around my neck; it was bigger than my previous one, which I was pleased about as it was starting to get a bit tight. My human told me I was to keep this one clean as I was to look smart at work; which also meant no rolling in chicken poo, which I was most upset about as it was one of my favourite things to do at the yard.

After the collar had been fitted, my name tag transferred, and a matching lead attached, I was placed in the car. As we drove along, I noticed that we were taking a different route than usual. The surroundings became more built-up around us, and the buildings changed from houses into shops and then to offices. We pulled into a space alongside many cars, in fact, the car park was far bigger than I had ever seen before, and there were people milling between cars and buildings all around me. As I stepped out of the car, excited at being somewhere new, I ran forward to sniff my way around. Once again, the lead kept my human at a constant distance behind me. She let me sniff around for a few moments: I could find no trace of other dogs being near, or any animals for that matter. In fact, the only things I could really smell were people and cars. There were a few small trees planted in some bark in between the cars and the fence-line, but everywhere else was boring tarmac. As I stood sniffing one of the trees, I became aware of a rumble in the distance. The sound quickly grew nearer, and before I knew it, the ground under me started to shake. I backed up to the safety of my human's legs and looked up to check for concern—but she didn't show any. My attention was quickly drawn back to the sound as it approached closer still, and then just the other side of the fence a large train, laden with great containers sped past on tracks that were hidden from my view. The noise was incredible and hurt my ears, the ground violently shook under my feet, and every part of me wanted to run and hide. But my owner, who remained calm and didn't pay attention to my panic, quickly soothed my anxiety. In fact, from that moment on, the trains passed frequently, and I soon learnt to ignore them completely.

After this, my human took the lead as I followed her away from the cars and around the building until we reached a door, above which the words, HEADWAY SUFFOLK were written. As soon as I walked through the door, I was met by a commotion of activity. There was a desk immediately in front of us as we walked in, behind which sat a bubbly receptionist who I would later get to know very well. In the corridor in front of me, many people were busily making their way into different rooms. Many of them wore a uniform consisting of black trousers and a blue cotton top with the same logo on the front as hung above the door. The other humans were all very different in appearance: some walked freely while some needed aids to help them. The one thing everyone had in common when they saw me was they all stopped and wanted to make a fuss. Despite slight anxiety over all the new sights and smells, my human remained calmly by my side and slowly introduced me to everybody. I learnt very quickly that the people within the building were either staff (who wore the uniform) or clients that came to Headway Suffolk for the day. I am ashamed to admit this now, but I remember vividly being very scared of some of the clients on my first day of work. Although my human was with me at all times and I felt safe with her, some of the clients were very different to all the other humans I had previously met. Some walked with sticks and some with frames, which made a noise every time the feet touched the floor. There were many wheelchairs, on which clients of different abilities were sat. Some were able to propel themselves along using large wheels on either side. The wheels were taller than I was and the direction it was going to turn was hard to read, unlike a human. Other clients sat on similar chairs but were unable to move themselves along. These clients required someone else to push them — usually a member of staff. Other chairs had smaller wheels and were powered by a large battery pack. These chairs were controlled by the user, and I quickly learnt they could be quite hard to control. The noise was also very unusual and took a lot of getting used to.

Besides the mobility, many of the clients also had other disabilities that quickly became apparent. Some had trouble talking and some even communicated via other methods, such as boards or through machines. Later on, I realised that my training would take all of this into consideration, but back then, I just tried to take it all in.

After lots of the humans had said hello to me, my human took me into a room opposite the reception desk for a bit of peace and quiet. Once the door had closed and the noise dulled, I was able to settle and take in the new surroundings. In the far corner was a desk on which there was a laptop, a printer, and other stationery, which made me realise it was an office. However, this was the only thing that made it like an ordinary office: on the far wall were many pictures of different dogs with their names written underneath. They were all different breeds or crossbreeds and not one looked like another. On another wall was a large chart, again pictures of different dogs that were placed in each section. Below the picture was their name with a small write up about the individual. Each dog had a list of commands with a checkbox to show whether they had learnt it yet or not. I had watched my human with Flo and Tilly and had picked up on certain words that they both seemed to understand. When I had asked Flo about them, she had sniggered at me and said, "You're not smart enough to learn anything yet." Hurt by the comment, I had asked Tilly the same question only a few days later. As usual, she sat down and took the time to explain to me that when I was old enough, my human would start teaching me what certain words meant. This was for our own safety and meant our human always had a way to tell us how to behave in different situations. Tilly also told me that sometimes our human would explain it wrongly, but I must always remain as patient with her as she would be to me.

Back in the room, I also noticed there were three cages like my one back at home, and some chairs lining the walls. In between two of the cages in the corner opposite the desk sat an unused washing machine—the use for this I wasn't to learn until a few years later. On top of the washing machine were two large boxes—one full of different treats, and the other was full to the brim with different toys. My human saw me looking at the box and took a soft pink rabbit from within and placed it on the floor for me to play with. I entertained myself while she busied herself on the laptop, and then, tired already from the stimulation of the morning, I curled up and went to sleep inside one of the crates.

I awoke to the sound of the door opening and saw two large men entering. They were both very different in appearance: the taller of two had tattoos covering his arms and neck and many piercings up both his ears. The other man was smaller in height and slimmer in his frame; he wore jeans and a t-shirt and bright red trainers. Both men seemed to recognise my human, and she greeted them warmly. I stretched myself out of the crate and went to say hello. Both men reached down to stroke me, and I was surprised at the gentleness of their touch — a far cry from the rough hands of the farmer. Once awake, my human seemed to sense my need to toilet, and she clipped my lead to my collar, and all four of us headed back outside to the barked area by the cars.

As soon as I was outside, I became distracted by a group of adults leaving an adjoining office. The youngest of the group, a female around my human's age, spotted me and came running over to see me. She giggled at my large ears and commented on how funny I looked — it had been a while since anyone had laughed at my appearance, and I felt a sharp pang inside - I didn't like it that people still thought I looked odd. I had forgotten all about needing the toilet since being outside, but it was evident my human had not. She seemed to understand that my brain was easily distracted, and I heard her explain exactly this to the two men. She politely explained to the lady that we must go and then headed over to the bark with me in tow. I turned back to see the lady still waiting where we left her, chuckling at the way I now waddled with my round belly and short legs. I wondered if I would ever grow into them.

Once I had finally relieved myself, we went back inside. The corridor was a lot quieter now, and the only person to make a fuss of me was the bubbly receptionist, who I later found out was named Caroline.

Back inside the room, my human retrieved a bag of small bone-shaped treats and sat with me on the floor: I was now about to learn my first command – 'SIT'.

Initially, all I could think about was the sweet-smelling treat that was placed lightly between my human's finger and thumb. I tried everything I could think of to get it; including scratching it out of her grasp, biting it, licking it, and finally jumping up and knocking it. However, every attempt quickly failed as my human clearly outsmarted me; holding it tightly enough so I didn't win but not too tight to break it. All the time, I was aware she was talking to the two men sat watching. After my attempts had failed, I started to watch a bit closer to what my human was doing, and I quickly noticed that the treat wasn't simply held in her hand. Instead, her hand started in front of my nose and slowly went up and slightly back. In noticing this, my head followed her hand, and as it went back, I felt my bottom hit the floor. Almost instantly when this happened, my human released the treat straight into my mouth taking me a bit by surprise. She then took another treat and repeated this over and over. Sometimes I would lose concentration and try and take the treat, but I quickly realised it was only as I placed my bottom on the floor that I would receive it. After I had successfully managed this a few times, my human started saying the word 'SIT' before moving her hand. I remembered back to hearing the commands spoken to Flo and Tilly and watching them do just as I was now – I had mastered it, my first command!!

Although extremely pleased with myself for understanding, I quickly became tired; the concentration had taken all my energy, and I was now torn between having more treats and going to sleep. However, my human again seemed to know how I was feeling, and I watched as she put the treat bag back in the box it had come from: a big smile on her face. Pleased with making her happy, I curled up in the crate and thought about what I had learnt: I couldn't wait to show Flo and Tilly.

As I laid there, I became aware of the door opening and a lady appeared in the doorway. She looked very smart in her pressed black trousers and white blouse. Her hair perfectly styled, and her makeup looked like she had come from a magazine. Her appearance was very different to my human, who always had hairs on her trousers from either myself or Flo. She picked clothes that didn't need ironing as she never seemed to have the time, and I had never seen her once wear makeup. Her hair was always tied up in the same bun that she had worn it on the first day I had seen her back at the farm. In fact, in the mornings when she was straight out of bed, it was still in the same style she had worn it the day before; many days, I'm not even sure if she found time to brush it, although she always swore to people she had.

As the posh lady came into the room, it was evident she had not even noticed the difference in their appearance. She shook my human's hand fondly and sat herself on one of the plastic chairs against the wall. I had seen her look at the material one that was closer, but despite lots of hoovering, it still had remnants of hair stuck to it from dogs that must have been there previous to me. As she sat down, I still felt tremendously sleepy, but I forced myself up to say hello. The lady who had previously been oblivious to my presence suddenly became overcome with 'oohs' and 'aahs'. Unperturbed by the fuss, which was now such a common occurrence, I made my way over until she had my head between her two beautifully manicured hands. She then proceeded to rub me so vigorously from side to side that my ears waved wildly and hit me back in the face. After I had taken as much as I could, I made my way back over to the bed to continue the rest I had been disturbed from; hoping that the ringing in my ears, caused by the over-exuberant fussing, would soon stop.

As I laid there, I found myself listening intently to the conversation unfolding between my human and the posh lady. It turned out she was a reporter and was interested in finding out more about the work of the 'BRAINY DOG SCHEME', of which I found out I was to play a part. I remember at the time hearing my name a lot and listening to how the scheme operated and what it was exactly that my human did for a job. I worked out why the room I was in smelled strongly of other dogs, and why everyone had been so excited at my arrival. However, at the time, I hadn't fully grasped exactly what it was I would be doing, for if I had, I might have tried harder to learn in those few months and become more of an asset to my human quicker.

However, just by listening to the two humans talking, I picked up a lot and will try my best now to recall what was said.

The building in which we were in had been specifically designed for the charity Headway Ipswich and East Suffolk, to whom my human was employed. At a later date (I'm not exactly sure when), the charity merged with another, becoming Headway Suffolk. I say I don't remember when as the exact date I'm not sure of. However, I do remember when it became finalised as I was invited to the celebration and I was apparently the star attraction!

I learnt how Headway Suffolk is a rehabilitation centre for clients with neurological conditions. They also provide many services outside of the centre for people in their own homes — however, I will get to these later.

Inside the centre, there were many rooms as well as the one in which we were sat. Each room was set up for different activities, which I found out included arts, history, IT, and my favourite — cooking; as well as many others that I can't remember. My human then went on to talk about other services, such as therapists and counselling, but I will admit, I switched off a bit with this as I couldn't really understand what was being said.

However, just as I was starting to doze, I heard my human say my name, and I instantly came back round. It was clear that she was now explaining more about the room that we were in as she started pointing to the photos on the wall. It was now that I really started paying attention.

I learnt that my human was the co-ordinator of a scheme called 'Brainy dogs,' which was another service that Headway Suffolk offered, not only to their clients, but anybody that suffered from a neurological condition.

All the dogs that were displayed on the walls were pictures of those that had been through the scheme already. They were either dogs that had been chosen and trained once a client had requested a dog, or they were dogs that already belonged to the clients but were at risk of being rehomed. At this point, my human pointed to a little beige hairy dog named 'LUNA' who she explained was a Pomeranian and had been the first dog to be rehomed through the scheme.

The dogs that were chosen for Headway clients were all selected from a rescue centre. I could see the posh lady had a moment of concern flick across her face, which my human had also picked up on:

"Rescue dogs often get a bad press, and people think they must be up for rehoming as there is something wrong with them. However, while we do not know the background to some of the dogs, most are there through no fault of their own. Their owners may have died or moved, or are simply working more hours than was fair on the dog. Therefore, they find themselves in a kennel looking for a new home. All of the dogs we have worked with are selected for their temperament and suitability to be placed with a specific client. This will be harder if we don't know the background to a dog but certainly doesn't mean they are dismissed from the selection."

She then went on to explain that the dogs were not trained to be assistance dogs. However, they were given training to be well-behaved companions and were there mainly to help clients with their emotional needs. I heard how many of the clients at Headway Suffolk had lost friends and even family, meaning they often became lonely and even depressed. By having a dog to share their life with, they would have something to get up in the morning for. They would also meet many people out on walks, and therefore, join what my human called a 'social network' again. At this point, I found myself remembering how my mother had told me my human would always come first, that I must put their needs before my own and always make them know they are the most important person in the world to me. Since being with my human, I had tried to do this, and I know how her face lit up when she saw me and Flo or Tilly. I also thought back to the time Tilly had told me it was our job to make our humans laugh when they are sad, to let them feel our warmth when they cry, and to enjoy their laughter when they are happy. I imagined how someone who had very few family and friends must feel if suddenly they had a dog who stuck to those rules. I imagined it would make the difference between happiness and sadness, and suddenly it hit me: my mother and Tilly were right—we had very important jobs to do, and I was going to do my hardest to do it to my very best ability.

However, after listening to my human, a moment of concern crossed my thoughts. Maybe I had gotten it wrong all this time. Maybe I wasn't really my human's, and I was just being trained for someone else. While I was sure my human would have only rehomed me to someone nice, the bottom line was I didn't want to go somewhere else: would I see Flo and Tilly again, would I ever get to meet Cuba, and what about my human — would I ever get to cuddle up to her again or feel her stroke my ears until I fell asleep?

However, I needn't have worried as my human then went on to talk about the other side of the scheme — and this is where my name was mentioned a lot.

As well as rehoming dogs to clients, my human wanted to start using dogs as a rehab tool for people that couldn't have their own. The theory behind this was that sometimes people relate to us dogs easier than other humans. They also have a higher motivation to work with us and so are more likely to do exercises and activities with us in a fun and rewarding way. My human explained that this is why I had been chosen, and the funny way she had handled me back at the farm was to check whether I was likely to be suitable for this kind of work. I also found out that in the future (and when I was ready), she was hoping to train me to do different things, so I could work alongside the clients and enhance their rehab to the full. At this stage, I wasn't sure what she meant but I looked forward to finding out, and the best thing was I would always belong to my human.

As my human went into more depth about what it was she had planned for me, I found my thoughts wandering to more concern. Up until this point, all I had ever heard was people laugh at me and say I was good for nothing. I remembered back to the visitors at the farm who had dismissed me when my brothers and sisters were there. Then there were the people who had come when I was the only one left: some had only looked at me before walking away shaking their heads. I remembered all the nasty comments about my appearance and even those that had pointed and laughed. I remembered the farmer hiding me away and his look of disappointment whenever he looked at me. If I am honest, back then, I had resigned myself to the fact that nobody would ever want me, and that I was just a big disappointment to everyone.

Now here I was listening to all these grand plans my human had for me. I heard her say how I would change the lives of many, and I was going to be a real asset to the scheme. While my human had never laughed at my appearance or seemed bothered in any way, I couldn't help feeling that she was putting too much faith in me. What if everyone was right; what if I really was good for nothing? All I was going to do was let my human down. I decided I only had one option- to try my hardest to not be a failure; I would put my heart and soul into everything I could, and I am pleased to say, looking back, that is exactly what I did.

Before the lady went, I heard my human explain that the two men who had come in earlier were there to help her train the dogs. They had come from a local open prison and came in every day. They were taught skills by my human in training the dogs, but it was their responsibility to make sure the dogs were trained correctly. In return, they gained skills that would help them later on in their life. I didn't know too much about what a prison was or what it meant about the two men, but so far, they had seemed kind and gentle, and to me, that was all that mattered—even if one of them still looked a bit scary with all the tattoos.

After the lady had gone, I fell into a deep sleep and processed everything I had learnt. I awoke abruptly to a loud crash followed by lots of shouting and general commotion. My human jumped to her feet before I had time to register the noise and stepped outside our room. The door caught on the edge of a chair leg creating a small gap that I could just about peer through. Just outside the door there was an abandoned wheelchair, which looked like it may have been the cause of the crashing noise that had woken me up. Stood next to the wheelchair was my human and two other members of staff. They were talking to a young gentleman (who was thrashing about the floor) in an attempt to calm him down. The man, who was clearly not in the mood to listen, continued to scream and scuttle across the floor. Initially, I thought he may have been injured after falling from his chair; however, I soon worked out that it was more likely he had thrown himself out in a fit of anger. He was clearly unable to walk; his legs fell lifelessly from his hips, his skin stuck to his bone from lack of any muscle. His arms, although clearly not completely mobile, were able to prop up his light body and mobilise him across the floor. From where I was sat, I could only see the man when he came in to view, but his screams echoed through me, making my head hurt. I struggled to understand what was going on, and I felt myself start shaking in fear. Never before had I seen someone so out of control, and his behaviour seemed so detached from any other human behaviour I had seen before. However, I watched as the staff proceeded to talk to the man until slowly but surely his manner changed, and he eventually made his way back over to the wheelchair where he was assisted back in.

My human who had remained by the door, out of the way but ready to assist, was now talking to one of the members of staff. I overheard her explain that the man only had funding for half a day but did not want to leave. His brain struggled to control his emotion, and the anger and upset he felt ended up being displayed as it had. Once he had been fully calmed, my human returned to the office where I was still sat shaking. She placed her hand gently on my head and once again soothed away my anxiety; although, I remained unsure about my ability to work with the clients after what I had just witnessed.

After my first day at work, my human took me to visit Tilly. I looked forward to telling her all about my day and everything I had learnt. After we had our mandatory play, we curled up on the rug, and Tilly listened to everything I had to tell her. She didn't interrupt me once, even when I went off on different tangents. I told her all about the car park, all the clients I saw, the staff I had met, the work of Headway Suffolk, the work I would be doing when I was grown up, and the client who had become very upset. I told her exactly how I was feeling too: how I was excited about learning lots of tricks, and how I wanted to help people. But I also explained how I had been scared of some of the clients, and how I was worried that I would be a failure.

After I had told Tilly absolutely everything, to the point that I thought I may have bored her to sleep, she finally began to speak. Her wise words once again soothed me, and I felt lucky to have such an astute friend to talk to.

She told me how she was proud of me for attending my first day, and I was right to be excited at what the future holds. She told me she had faith that I would do my human proud in whatever it was she asked of me. She spoke to me about the other dogs, and the posh lady, and everything else I had spoken to her about. But when it came to addressing me being scared, I could see the muscles of her jowls tighten, and a look of solemnity flick across her eyes.

"Nobody on this planet has the right to judge others. Nobody knows what others are feeling, or have walked the same path in the same shoes. Humans can be some of the kindest animals you will ever meet, their intelligence outweighs ours second to none.

However, with their sharp brain comes the process of judgement, prejudice, and social norms. I have been on this earth 11 years, and I have witnessed children being bullied in the street because they aren't wearing the right shoes, or their hair looked funny. I have heard adults arguing in cars about whose is worth more and should, therefore, move over so they could pass; and I have seen people using wheelchairs being stared at and name called because they aren't able to walk on their legs like the others.

Humans can be spiteful and horrid to each other, and friendships can fall apart at the drop of a hat. We, as dogs, are lucky in that our brains work differently to our humans. While initially, you may be scared of things you haven't seen before, you must not mistake this for judgement. The next time you see it, you will not be scared and, therefore, you must treat it no differently to anything else. As dogs, all we must care about is being treated fairly; we must look forward to the hands that are kind to us and be wary of those that are not. But we must accept that accidents happen and be prepared to forgive many times over before truly accepting we may be wary.

You will be lucky in your job as you will be the one that will truly not judge those that have been judged by others. You will learn over time to tell which way the wheelchair will turn and, therefore, treat it no differently to a person walking next to you. You will learn to understand those that cannot speak as well as others, and you will find a way to communicate with them just as easily as those that can. You will treat everybody the same no matter what their appearance or social status. In return, you will find that you become the one people turn to and look forward to seeing, and you will be able to hold your head higher than any human around you.

You, yourself, know what it feels like to be judged. You have had humans judge you from the moment you were born. They decided, without even knowing you, that you would be worthless and no good, purely on the way you were put together. You, Hope, can relate to these humans more than our human can. You have the power to make a difference, simply by not judging: by seeing everyone as the same.

And for the record, the humans were wrong to judge you. Our human saw more in you than those that judged you — and she had good reason. You have a heart that is purer than any other dog I have had the pleasure of meeting — and trust me, I've met a few. I don't doubt that you will do our human proud — and I know that when the time comes, I will be safe leaving her in your capable paws."

And with that, she laid her wise old head across my shoulder blades before muttering under her sleepy breath, "You are going to be one special dog, Hope, one special dog indeed." She then closed her eyes and went to sleep.

I laid there for a while taking in everything she had said. I thought back to all the people I had met today and pondered about how I had been scared of some. I wondered if I had shown my fear, and in doing so, let Tilly down. She had such high hopes for me, and I feared more of letting her down than I did my human. I wished that I could take her to work with me, that I could see her work her magic with the clients as I had often seen her do with my human. I wondered why my human had chosen me and not Tilly for this job; but as I looked at her sleeping beside me, I noticed how old she was starting to look and remembered her comments about her not being here forever. Then suddenly it hit me — Tilly may not have as long left here with me as I had hoped. And with that, I forgot about work and all the people and what the future might bring, for I realised it may not all be good. So I snuggled in closer to the warmth next to me. Even while she slept, she had a way of making everything better, and I found myself dozing off, and there we stayed until my human carefully lifted me sleepily back to the car and then home. Tomorrow would be another day at work, and I promised myself tomorrow, and the day after, and the day after that, that I would never forget Tilly's wise words—and they are words that still ring true with me today.

Starting to feel all grown up

GROWING UP

In the months after starting work, I found I started to grow up quickly. More so in what I learnt and how I thought but also in my appearance. It was a gradual process, but over time, I started to change shape, and I noticed people stopped commenting on me so much. The main thing that changed was my legs started to grow, and I lost my big round belly. My body started to fit the big paws it was supported on, and I started to look more in proportion. I grew a neck, and while my ears remained long in relation to my head, they no longer flopped awkwardly in front of my legs. I found I no longer waddled when walking, and as my legs grew taller, I found I could actually run without the risk of tripping over every few strides. In fact, rather than being embarrassed to run, I started to really enjoy it, and I practised everywhere I could. My favourite place to practice was up at the yard: once Cuba was safely stabled for the night and my human was picking up the poo in the field, Flo and I would run until our heart's content in the big, wide, open field. Sometimes during the day, I would sit and watch Cuba; the way she floated above the ground, tail streaming behind her, and I wished I could look as graceful as she did.

I was still very young when I first properly met her. I had been going to work with my human for about a week, and we would go to the yard before and after on most days. I had always remained in the car when my human was leading her to and from the field. However, on this particular day, Flo had come up with us as it was a day we did not go to work. Flo had met Cuba many times, but had told me numerous times she had no interest in getting to know her. However, she did know the 'rules' as my human put it, and was to teach me how to stay safe.

As my human slipped the large head collar over her ears and led her out of the stable, I was taken aback as to just how big she was. I watched as her feet hit the floor with every step she took and made a note to myself to stay well away—there was no way I wanted one of them landing on me. From down here, her legs looked like elegant tree trunks, reaching up to support a strong muscly frame. As she walked away, I could see her muscles ripple under her glossy coat, the sun reflecting off each black hair individually creating a shine I could only dream of. My human was only as tall as her back, and from her powerful shoulders reached a thick neck on which was set her beautiful head. She had long flowing hair from between her ears, which fell down her nose covering her eyes, and her tail streamed out behind her, swinging from side to side with every step. I stood transfixed for a while as she walked politely next to my human's side. Her head was up, ears pricked forward, and she was clearly alert to everything going on around her. She had a way about her that screamed importance, elegance, and most of all, respect.

Suddenly, I realised that in my state of awe, they had walked halfway to the field, Flo trotting safely behind. Without thinking, I ran forward to catch up. Cuba must have seen me running behind her—a stranger in her eyes; and I saw her ears flick forward and backwards and her legs start to dance in concern. Before I managed to get too close, Flo stopped in her tracks, turned sideways and blocked my path

"Never go behind her," She glared, before shaking her head and continuing on.

I looked up to see my human, hand gently stroking Cuba's strong neck, turning to see where I was. On seeing I was at a safe distance, she continued back towards the field, Cuba once again settled beside her. My first lesson in horse etiquette was complete.

After that, I was allowed out at all times up the yard. I stayed with Flo when my human was leading Cuba, and she seemed happy to accept me following on behind at a safe distance. When she was in her stable, I took the time to get to know her over the door. To start with, she appeared just as unsure of me as I was of her, which I found odd considering how much bigger she was than me. She would stretch her long neck over the top of the door and bring her head down until it was at my level. From here, I could see her bright eyes from under her hair, and I could see her intelligence shining through. Initially, despite wanting to get acquainted, we would both pull away before actually touching. However, over the days and weeks that followed, we both became braver until she would let me touch her velvety muzzle, and in return, she would breathe warm air into my ears. It became a mutual friendship; no words were ever spoken, but a ritual greeting between us.

Alongside Cuba, my friendships also grew with the other dogs at the yard. The two Alsatians were not concerned with making friends and so I never pushed this – but some of the Jack Russells were great fun. My favourite was Jamie, and we would make many great games together. Our favourite of all was called 'dodge' and involved running as fast as we could without slowing down when something was in our path. At this point, we would have to dodge the object and continue on. Now this sounds quite easy, but when you have lots of other dogs, horses, children, adults, and chickens that suddenly appear in your path, it becomes a lot harder. In addition to this, the driveway was made from shingle, which would slip and slide under our feet making sharp turns somewhat difficult. When we first started playing this game, Jamie was always much better than me: he was lighter on his feet and could manage the sharp turns easily. I, on the other hand, quite often ended up running into somebody's leg where I had misjudged their pace or sliding completely over on the shingle. One time, we decided to have a race the entire way around the yard and kennel blocks. Jamie had slightly taken the lead after an impressive dodge around the cockerel at the far end of the yard. We had a long run past the kennels until the finish line, and the route was clear: making it my only chance to overtake and win. I pushed myself as hard as I could and overtook Jamie about halfway along. I turned around to check he wasn't likely to catch me, and when I looked back, I was nearing the corner back to the car park. Before I knew it, four little legs appeared around the corner, which I knew belonged to two children whose mother had a horse at the yard. I tried to stop, but the speed which I had been going at caused my back feet to skid past my front feet; my legs were now in a position where it would have been impossible for me to create a dodge, and I ended up bowling into both sets of legs at once. The children were sent backwards with the force and landed with a heavy thump on their backs, quickly followed by loud crying, which alerted all the adults to what had happened. My human was one of the first on the scene along with the children's mother, and I was very quickly scolded for being so careless. After that, Jamie and I never played dodge again, although he would remind me of it on many occasions.

In addition to the yard, I started to make friends out on walks. My favourite place to go to meet new friends was a local common area by the beach. We would quite often go here when Flo was able to come with us as it was close to the beach but meant she didn't need to go on the stones. Lots of dogs from all around would come here, and I never once knew it to be quiet.

Most of the time, Flo would keep herself to herself and kept her distance from the other dogs. She had made it clear from day one that she had no interest in playing with dogs she didn't know, and even those she did most of the time. I, on the other hand, loved meeting new friends and would go out of my way to say hello. The only problem was with making friends this way was you rarely ever saw them again. Sometimes I wondered whether this was actually the reason why Flo didn't want to make socialise, in case she became attached, but she soon made it clear that this was not the case:

"I merely do not wish to socialise with other dogs, I have no reason to. I do not see it as fun to run around in circles with someone I have just met when I could be spending time playing with our human or chasing rabbits. Besides which, there are many dogs that do not mean well, they have been poorly socialised, and as such, do not play as you would like. I have seen it when dogs have been playing well together and then WHAM, one has turned, and the other is held in a deathly lock within its jaws. I will not do harm to another dog, but again, do not expect me to waste my time with those I do not know."

I had many points I wanted to raise with her after this, but I could see it was not the time. I was also sure that part of the reason she didn't wish to play with others was because of her back, although she would never admit to this — so it was pointless asking.

Sometimes when we were out together, and I found another dog to play with, it was awkward having Flo there too. She would quite often grumble if we went anywhere near her, and a lot of dogs wouldn't play with me because of it. Initially, I found this really annoying and even started to resent Flo being with me. I tried to ask her if she could go away when I found someone to play with, but she always refused. I thought she was just being awkward to start with and wondered if she enjoyed ruining my fun. One day, after yet again another dog told me they would go and find someone else to play with (as it was clear Flo didn't want them there), I asked Flo why she couldn't just let me play by myself. She merely replied

"Because, one day, you might need me."

Now, so far in my life, I had never met a horrible dog, or one that didn't want to play (apart from Flo that is), so I struggled to see why she believed there were nasty dogs about. But it wasn't long after that that I came to realise she was right.

We were walking one of our usual routes by our house. It wasn't one of my favourites as we rarely met anyone else along it. Flo liked it though as one side of the track was lined with trees that stretched back quite a distance. In here, there were often strong scent marks of other animals, and occasionally squirrels and rabbits would run past which she couldn't resist but chase. On the other side of the track was a large field. Most of the time, it was off limits with crops growing, but once these had been harvested, the stubble made a great place to run.

We were about halfway along when I saw a dog in the distance, its human walking a little way behind. As we got closer, I could see it was a crossbreed like myself, but I struggled to work out what breeds its parents were likely to be, which I remembered Tilly telling me once was called a mongrel. It was taller than me but was quite slim in the frame. It was black and had a long scruffy hair, which I thought could have done with a brush. As we got closer, Flo moved herself into the stubble field, so she didn't have to socialise, and I trotted forward to say hello. The dog was standing still and watching me with piercing eyes, but at the time, I didn't think anything of it. Before I had even managed to get close enough to introduce myself, the dog ran forward snapping and snarling at me. I had no time to react, and before I knew it, I had been bowled over between its front paws and could feel its teeth pressing into the scruff of my neck. I was so scared I didn't dare move, and I remember closing my eyes waiting for its teeth to pierce my skin: but it never happened. The next thing I was aware of was a force hitting the side of us; knocking the mongrel from its grip. I remained crouched to the floor and watched as Flo and the mongrel rolled around in a web of teeth snapping and growling. I had never seen this side of Flo before, and despite being so much smaller, she put up a good fight. I remember laying there petrified as to what might happen to her as the mongrel narrowly missed her many times; and at the same time, I was extremely grateful that she had been there, as promised, to protect me. They must have only been fighting for a moment before the two humans ran in and managed to prise them apart, but it felt like an eternity. After the mongrel was safely back on its lead and my human had checked both Flo and me over for injuries, the two humans exchanged words about the incident. The mongrel's owner apologised profusely and said he had been in a few 'scuffles' as she called it before. At this point, my human calmly but firmly pointed out that other walkers should be warned so they can keep their dogs away, which she said she would do. As we started walking away, I noticed Flo was walking with a limp on her front leg. I tried to ask her if she was ok and to thank her for looking after me, but she just looked at me and said

"And that, Hope, is what I've been warning you about."

After that incident, I have been much more wary when going to greet other dogs, and I have never once moaned about Flo staying nearby again. In fact, if I'm entirely honest, I now feel much safer when she is there.

I also learnt a lot at work, and the list of commands I started to know continued to grow. After I had mastered 'sit,' I found I was asked to do it everywhere, which my human said would help me with my manners. I was to sit to have my lead on, my lead off, before going through doors, and at the curbs. To start with, I found this hard as I would become distracted by things, and to be honest, I didn't really see the point. However, my human and the guys that were helping train me were much more stubborn than I was, and I soon learnt that I wasn't going to get where I wanted to go unless I did it. I was also always rewarded with a treat once I had done it, which made it worth my while.

After this, I was taught to lie down. Again, a treat was used, which I followed with my nose from a sitting position down towards the floor. Now I had learnt from when I was taught sit that trying to just take the treat didn't work; so I knew I had to do something before it would be released from the human. However, to start with, I followed the treat down with my nose until my ears flopped in front of my eyes. I heard the humans saying this was good, but the treat still wasn't being released. After this had happened a few times, I felt a hand on the top of my shoulder blades. Initially, I thought they were going to stroke me, which I thought was odd in the middle of training—and to be honest, I was much more interested in the treat than I was a stroke. But the hand remained on the top of my shoulders, and I felt some pressure being applied behind it. Although the pressure was far from hurting me, it wasn't very pleasurable and so I ducked my shoulders away from it. This movement, along with my nose following the treat made my whole body move until my front legs were in front of me and my stomach touched the floor. As soon as this happened, I found the human's hand released the treat, and I was able to take it. Again, this was repeated many times and the command 'down' was spoken. After a while, I no longer needed the pressure on my shoulders, and I learnt that if I simply followed the treat and lowered my body in the same way I had been doing, that the treat was released just as easily. Over the following days, I found that the treat was moved further from my nose, but the same motion was applied by the human's hands. I thought maybe they had made a mistake and forgotten what we had been doing, so I moved forward so my nose was touching their hand again. However, this seemed to frustrate the humans, and they kept moving back so they were further away. After I had tried this a few times, I realised that they seemed to be doing it on purpose, although I couldn't work out why. So the next time they did it, I stayed where I was and lowered my body as I had been doing. This seemed to make them very happy, and they leant forward and popped the treat in my mouth. After that, no matter how far back they were or even if they were standing, if I saw them point their hand to the floor and say the word 'down', I would do exactly that, and I was always rewarded with a treat – 'Bingo', my second command was mastered.

As with the sit, I was asked to lie down in a variety of places until my human was sure I would do it anywhere. Most of the places, I didn't mind, but it took a while for me to get over the feeling of lying down in the park. I don't think my human was very pleased at first, as every time I went down, the grass tickled my belly and my natural instinct was to stand back up. However, after I had done this a few times, and I could see a look of disappointment cross my humans face, I remembered what Tilly and my mother had told me about humans knowing best, and so I put my discomfort to one side. To be honest, I soon got over the feeling anyway, and it wasn't long until the grass felt the same to lie on as the office floor or the sofa (although the sofa was always that bit more comfy).

After this, I was then taught a few more commands, which included stay, fetch, and walking nicely on a lead. I found learning stay was the easiest of the lot, as all I had to do was literally stay wherever I was, and my human would walk away and then walk back to me and give me a treat. To be completely honest, to start with, I thought there was going to be more to it than that, but there never was. The only time I found it hard was when my human went out of sight. I never usually let her out of my sight as I was always worried I would lose her—which I learnt the hard way when I had just started being let off my lead.

We were out for a walk, Flo had stayed at home because her back had been hurting and so she wanted to rest. My human had driven us to a local wood where I had never been before. As soon as I got out of the car, I was overwhelmed by all the smells: there were squirrel tracks, mice, rabbits, and even deer. The ground had a damp feel and smell to it, and the leaves had just fallen, which made great fun to run through. I had been playing in a pile of fallen leaves when I saw a movement out of the corner of my eye- a squirrel! I had seen Flo chasing them before, and she always told me it was her ambition to catch one before it made its way safely up a tree. Now, at this age, I was still very determined to make Flo like me, and I imagined catching the squirrel and impressing her so much that she would see me as a great friend—so off I set. I chased it down the path, around a corner, and through some trees until I saw it scamper up a tree quite a way from where I was. Disheartened, I turned back to find my human who I had left behind and was now completely out of sight. I found my way back to the path and followed it back the way I had come until I found the spot where I had last left her: but she was nowhere to be seen. I remember the feeling of dread come over me more quickly than I could ever have imagined. I stood and looked around, my ears pricked as high as I could make them to try and hear any sign of her — but there was none. I ran back a bit further in case I had misjudged where I left her, then I turned and ran further along the track in case I had missed her go past — but there was still no sign of her. I lifted my nose to the air and tried to find her scent, but I hadn't developed that skill very well, and I couldn't distinguish one smell from the other. The panic started to rise inside, and I had no clue what to do, when all of a sudden, I saw a movement behind a large tree that was just off the track. I stood and watched transfixed, was it her? Or was it someone else who was lying in wait to steal me? In those split seconds, so many thoughts crossed my mind: do I run? Do I stay? Will I ever see my human again? What about Tilly and Flo? If I run, will I ever find my way home? What if my human was looking for me, and I ran away? But then, the figure stepped out from behind the tree: my human, with a giant grin cross her face. Part of me wanted to be mad that she found my panic so amusing, but I was so relieved I had found her, that I forgave her instantly. I promised myself there and then that I would never let her out of my sight again.

When I next saw Tilly, I told her about what had happened in the woods. She told me the exact same thing had happened to her when she was my age; and she, too, had decided never to let her out of her sight again. Then she went quiet, and I could see she was thinking hard

"Do you know what Hope? I think she has done it on purpose- to scare us so we never run out of sight again."

And then she chuckled to herself.

"Sometimes we don't give our humans enough credit."

And then she chuckled some more.

Ever since that day, I kept my promise to myself. I did not care if my human had scared me on purpose or not: there was no way I ever wanted to lose her again, and if that meant walking by her side forever more, then so be it.

So when I was learning out of sight waits, I found it very hard to remain where I was- as I'm sure you can imagine. I was torn between my desire to be obedient, and my need to keep my human in sight. Initially, I found it too difficult, and as soon as I couldn't see her, I would go and find her. However, she was always insistent I went back and sat where I had just been. She would then try again. After a few attempts, my human sat me back and went out of sight — but this time only for a split second. I didn't even have time to stand up before she was back in sight and walking over to me with a treat. I didn't really realise what was going on until she did it again, and again, and again: each time, staying out of sight that tiny bit longer. Although I was desperate to go find her, I learnt that she would always come back and reward me; and the small stages she took out of sight were just about bearable. One time, I even waited for a whole minute until she came back into sight — I received a really big reward for this, so I know she must have been pleased — which always meant more to me than the treat anyway.

As for the 'walking on a loose lead,' I picked that up very quickly. I never really wanted to be far from my human anyway. Occasionally I would get excited and be in a rush to get somewhere. In these instances, my human (or the guys if I was at work) would either stop or turn back and walk a few steps in the other direction. I soon learnt that I would get where I wanted much quicker if I remained calm and didn't pull forward.

There was one dog who came in for training who used to pull his humans everywhere. His name was Bob, and he was a mastiff cross: and he made Tilly look puny in comparison. I remember being very scared when I first met him as he was almost as broad as he was long. His shoulders were like boulders, and his muscles rippled as he walked. His neck was almost as wide as his chest, and his head was three times the size of mine. He oozed confidence when he walked, and consequently, had no regard for his human being pulled along behind him. I watched as my human and the guys worked with him on his first day. He had no interest in the treats being offered and walked wherever he wanted to go. Any corrections my human tried to make had no impact on his thick neck or he simply refused to acknowledge them. Over time, I watched him improve, and he paid the humans more and more respect; I think it helped that when he was good, he was always allowed to have a game with his ball which he loved.

Once he was able to concentrate on his own, I was then brought in to work alongside him; it was in these times that I learnt he wasn't at all scary, and was, in fact, one of the nicest dogs I had ever met. We spent many hours working together with lots of different activities; my human said it was good for us to work alongside other dogs, so we learnt to concentrate on our humans and ignore what was going on around us. While the activities were hard and required lots of concentration, both Bob and I tried our hardest. We had to walk towards each other in different directions, making sure we didn't look at each other as we passed; we had to walk in a circle, spiralling in to each other, again keeping our attention fully on our handler; we had to sit or lie dead still while the other walked or ran past, and finally, we had to stay while the other dog was recalled away back to their handler. Bob became very good with all the activities, and my human was very pleased with his progress. However, when his owner became involved with the training, it was clear things weren't as simple as first thought. While Bob walked very nicely on the lead now and no longer pulled wherever he wanted to go, he only had to lean down to sniff something and he nearly pulled her over. It was clear that Bob didn't mean to pull, but he was so big and powerful; combined with his humans' poor balance, it was a recipe for disaster. His human was so keen to walk him, though, that she was not going to be defeated: and neither was my human. In the end, they found a piece of equipment that fitted around Bob's nose and tied up behind his ears. The lead attached to this instead of the collar and meant Bob couldn't put his head down to sniff, for if he did, his nose was simply pulled back around. To start with, Bob didn't like the new piece of equipment and would constantly try and get it off. However, over time, he admitted it wasn't as bad as he originally thought. He learnt he could still sniff things, he just had to be a bit more mindful about how he did it. He also said it was worth it as he was now able to spend a lot more time with his human. The last time I ever saw Bob was as he walked out of the office beside his human—both with beaming smiles as they went.

EVERYBODY NEEDS HOPE

Me at 8 months old

LOSS OF A LOVED ONE

When I was a year old, my human went away. It was the first time I had ever been left, and I didn't understand what was going on. It started with piles of clothes all over the living room, and a large bag that I had never seen before. She would put clothes from different piles into the bag, then take them out, then put other ones in, and so on. I sat and watched for a while but quickly became bored.

"You know what this means, don't you?" Flo skulked……. "She's going away and leaving us."

I obviously went in to complete meltdown at this point—how could she leave us? What had I done wrong? Had I not done well enough at work? How could I try harder? What did I need to do to persuade her not to leave?

All these thoughts and many others went through my mind, but I couldn't think of an answer to any of them. Distraught, I curled up in my bed and tried to believe that Flo was wrong, maybe she had made it up just to be horrid. But one look at her solemn face told me she wasn't. I watched as the packing continued until the bag was filled: zip nearly busting open. Then my human turned to our things: toys were picked up, bowls washed, food placed into bags, and then the bed was taken near enough from underneath me, and everything was placed into the car. One final check around, and before I knew it, Flo and I were placed into the boot without a chance to argue.

As we travelled in silence, I became more and more aware of the feeling of dread inside my stomach—where were we going? Would I ever see my human again? As we drove along, I took no notice of where we were going and was surprised to feel the car slow up outside Tilly's house. Here, all of mine and Flo's things were unloaded and taken inside the house where my human's mother stood waiting. Sombrely, we followed our human inside the house, still unsure of what was going on. Tilly greeted me from inside and instantly picked up on my worry. She followed me into her living room where I laid and watched my human talking to her mother. She seemed to be explaining different things she had brought in from the car, and every now and again, would look up and point at either myself or Flo, who was also sulking beside me in the living room. Tilly asked what was wrong, and when I explained what Flo had told me, Tilly turned to Flo and shook her head.

"Yes, sometimes our humans go away—but what Flo has omitted to tell you is that she will come back. Every now and again, they go away—sometimes you are lucky enough to go with them, but sometimes we have to stay behind and wait for them to return."

On hearing this, I felt instantly relieved and was thankful once again for Tilly. As she walked back out to be with the humans, I couldn't help but notice how she was dragging a back leg. I followed on behind leaving Flo still sulking in the living room. I stood beside Tilly as my human said her goodbyes to us all and then made her way back into the car. We stood and watched as the car drove out of sight, and then my human's mother closed the door, and I suddenly felt all alone.

My human's parents did a lot for me and Flo while we stayed with them, and it was clear they tried to make us feel at home. They took us for walks, played with us in the garden, and sometimes even sat on the floor and cuddled us as we weren't allowed on their furniture. However, the only thing that really helped me get through that time without my human was Tilly. She would play with me during the day and would cuddle up to me at night. When I was feeling especially lonely, she would take the time to tell me stories about my human from when they were both younger.

Out of all the stories she told me, my favourite was the time she was lucky enough to go on a holiday with my human and her parents. She was placed alone in the boot while the rest of the car was filled to the brim with luggage and other belongings. They travelled for many hours, stopping a couple of times to allow Tilly to stretch her legs and alleviate herself before finally arriving at the Lake District. Tilly described the scenery as she stepped out of the car. There was greenery everywhere and not another house for miles. Sheep roamed the fields freely, and the fields turned into mountains that stretched high above the clouds. The house they stayed in was a beautiful old farmhouse with large rooms and an open fire place. The furniture was old, and as Tilly was on holiday too, she was treated to resting on a large sofa that stretched under the window. In the morning, the fields were often hazy as a light fog filled the air, obscuring the mountains from view. As the morning went on, the fog lifted, and the bright sunshine would penetrate the clouds bringing the scenery to life.

Tilly went on to explain about the walks she would go on with our human and her parents. The walks would often go on for many hours and would take them up and over the mountains that surrounded the farmhouse. On the trails, Tilly saw many wild sheep and would often come across carcasses from those that had grown tired from old age or had unfortunate accidents on the precarious mountain ledges. She saw birds of prey circling above the fresher carcasses and even saw foxes that preyed on the weak lambs that had just been born. At the top of the mountain, they would all sit and enjoy the wondrous views below; the humans restoring their energy with drinks and snacks. They always brought something for Tilly to enjoy and had fresh water contained within bottles. However, where possible, Tilly preferred to drink from the freshwater streams that made their way down the side of the mountains, or from the lakes that filled in the plateaus.

After the lengthy walks, they would often stop at the local pub where the humans would engage with other walkers over a large glass of something cold. Tilly enjoyed meeting other dogs that had also been lucky enough to go along with their owners.

Occasionally, Tilly and my human would go off by themselves and explore the smaller walks. One day, they went out early morning and found a small deserted farmhouse hidden from view by the overgrown hedges. In the privacy of the forgotten land, they sat together and basked in the warm sunshine. My human fell asleep for many hours and awoke only when the sun had gone behind the mountain top, creating a chill in the air. Tilly had enjoyed their time alone together and had laid loyally by her side. While our human slept peacefully on, Tilly had kept watch for signs of any danger. When they finally made their way back to the farmhouse, they were met by her worried parents who thought she may have had an accident on the mountainside—they were banned from going out exploring on their own after that.

As Tilly reminisced about her time in the Lake District, I could see a look of remorse in her eyes. She had been in her prime back then, and the walks had been easy. Nowadays, her bones grumbled with exercise despite her young brain wishing she was still competent. She spoke about the way she had leapt across boulders and sprinted through the streams. She had helped our human up the steeper parts of the trails and raced her down the other side. It was clear that they had been the best of friends, and I could tell how Tilly longed to be that young fit and healthy dog once again.

Another time, after I had been telling her about my latest tricks I had learnt at work, Tilly told me about the time she went to work with our human. However, it wasn't the same place as where I went and must have been a previous job. Tilly was about eight, and my human no longer lived with her as she had moved out of her parent's house. I didn't have to ask Tilly how she felt about this as her expression said it all. She did say that our human always made time to come and see her though, and they still went out on many adventures, just the two of them.

Tilly wasn't sure why she had been taken to the work place, but she remembered going like it was yesterday. The outside was grand and had many windows stretching up to three floors. As they went in, they were greeted by a receptionist, just like at Headway Suffolk. However, as Tilly explained the rest of the building, it was clear this was the only similarity. Leading off from the reception area was a long hallway that went off in both directions. Tilly only went down one way, which led to some stairs at the end, so she wasn't sure what was down there. However, she guessed it was more rooms like she passed on the way to the stairs. Apart from one big room, which was filled with chairs and a large TV, the rest of the rooms were smaller and had a bed, a desk, a wardrobe, and some drawers. Some of the rooms had people lying in their beds, but most people seemed to be in large comfy chairs in the corner. Tilly didn't have time to see any more of the rooms as she was taken up the stairs and through a locked door, which had the words 'Dementia Unit' written above. The layout was the same as the floor below, but the atmosphere was very different. As they passed the rooms, Tilly noticed some of the humans laid in their beds quietly, large cushioned pads lined the high sides making an adult-sized cot. Many of the humans wandered up and down the corridors, while others, sat in a large room at the end. Tilly was taken into the room and introduced to the humans sitting there. Some were unmoved while others were clearly ecstatic at her presence. Tilly told me how she noticed our human's reaction with one resident in particular. She was a frail old lady who Tilly was taken in to see after she had said hello to everyone in the main lounge. She was in a bedroom at the end of the corridor. As Tilly approached the room, she could hear wailing from within and was unsure about what she would encounter when she entered. The bed had sides up like she had seen in some of the other rooms, however, the pads were not neatly placed like they had been on others, but there had clearly been an attempt to remove them. The Velcro holding them on still only doing its job in places. Over the side of the pad, two bony legs and feet were protruding out at a strange angle and kicked about restlessly. Tilly could not see the human inside the bed but could still hear the wailing coming from within. She sat patiently while our human leant gently over the side of the bed and spoke calmly to the human inside. She dropped Tilly's lead to the floor and assisted the person (who Tilly could now see was an elderly woman) into a sitting position in the bed. The lady was very frail, and Tilly remembers her bones clearly protruding from under her skin. Her hair was white and fuzzy and stuck out wildly in all directions from her head. The lady was clearly unsettled and quickly tried to wriggle her way back down the bed. However, in doing so, she spotted Tilly sitting patiently by the bedside and, instantly, she stopped. She moved her body over to the side of the bed and waved her hand over the side. As if on cue, Tilly moved forward and placed her head under the bony hand. She felt the fingers of the lady move awkwardly to begin with, but then instinct took over, and the movement became fluid and relaxed. Tilly said how she could physically feel the lady ease as she stroked her. The anxiety and restlessness she had felt earlier seemed to leave her body as she continued to feel the warmth of Tilly's head under her fingers. Tilly became aware of two figures standing behind her in the doorway but didn't want to turn and look in case she upset the lady who was now calm and relaxed. Our human, however, spoke to them, and Tilly could work out they were carers on shift at the time. They all seemed amazed at the transformation in the lady, who by all accounts, was always restless despite many attempts from staff to calm her. After Tilly had been sat there for a while, one of the carers brought in a plate of food for the lady. The food had clearly been blended into soft mush, and it was at this point, Tilly noticed the lady had no teeth. Our human slowly moved Tilly to the side, so she was out of reach of the lady but was still in plain sight. The other carer moved a chair up to where Tilly had been and began to feed the lady. The lady ate every spoonful that was placed near her lips, but she never once took her eyes from Tilly. Tilly, as usual, remained patient next to our human's side as she spoke to the carer who had been feeding the lady. Tilly heard how she was usually so restless that she would refuse most of the meal, which resulted in her severe weight loss. Again, the carers had tried all they could to encourage eating and had even tried weight-gain drinks; however, this had resulted in the carer at the time wearing the drink that was thrown in disgust by the lady. It seemed that Tilly's mere presence had such a powerful effect on the lady that was impossible to ignore.

Apparently, after that day, the home in which Tilly had visited paid for weekly dog visits to benefit all of the patients. The lady had a large realistic stuffed dog bought for her, which now sat proudly at the bottom of the bed. The lady, herself, still had days when she was upset, but our human told Tilly how she had made a real difference to the quality of the ladies life, and for that, she would always be grateful.

After Tilly's visit, our human had found it impossible to forget the impact that Tilly had had on the residents. She told Tilly it was this that sparked her enthusiasm to use dogs as a therapeutic and rehab tool for people: which in turn, had led her to purchase of Flo, and then me.

As Tilly told me all these stories from her past, I tried to imagine what she would have looked like in her prime years. I had seen pictures on the wall, but as I looked at the ageing body in front of me, I found it hard to envisage the powerful creature she once was. In fact, as I laid there next to her, I thought back to the dog I had met only a year ago, and I realised there had already been a huge deterioration. Her entire face was now grey (including her eyebrows), and she had white hairs up all four of her legs. She had grown little warts across parts of her body, and her coat had lost all of its shine. One of her back legs had not only become arthritic but had nerve damage, which resulted in the dragging of the leg I had noticed earlier in the week. The same leg had consequently lost all of its muscle tone and looked weak and feeble compared to the others. She had also grown very tired of late, and while she still tried to play, it wasn't long before her legs failed her, and she was forced to stop. If she tried to ignore her grumbling body, she would find walking the next day even more painful. She would usually try and brush it under the carpet, and it wasn't until now, that I thought about it, and I realised she was probably in a lot of pain on those days. I had noticed my human's parents add something to her food while I had been here, and she always seemed happier a little while after eating, and I wondered if the treatment was some kind of pain relief.

In the days that followed after this, I no longer asked Tilly to play with me, instead, if I was bored, I would take a ball out into the garden by myself. I had only thrown it around a few times when I felt Tilly come up beside me. She picked the ball up and threw it for me to catch. Uneasy about encouraging her to play, I stayed where I was, however, she took one look at me and muttered

"There's nothing wrong with me!" and nodded over towards the ball. I ran to fetch it as instructed, and before long, we were playing like we always had done. For a while, I forgot all about my concern as I leapt around the garden after the ball, which at this point, had been flung into the middle of a beautifully trimmed hedge. On my return, I noticed Tilly was standing with her back leg curled awkwardly underneath her, the top of her foot resting on the ground. Unaware, she took a step forward to meet me and her leg dragged across the ground behind, ripping the top of her nails as she did so.

Flo, who had been sitting in the sunshine this whole time, suddenly jumped forward and grabbed the ball from between my legs. She turned around to Tilly who was still completely unaware of the damage to her foot:

"My turn now."

And she nodded subtly for Tilly to look behind where there was now a small trail of blood oozing from her nails. Tilly nodded in acknowledgement and limped back inside where she sat and cleaned her back foot as best as she could.

Every part of me wanted to run in and see if she was alright, but Flo told me to give her space. I knew Tilly was in denial about her age, and Flo was right, she would be embarrassed about what had just happened. I had a lot more respect for Flo after that day.

The next day, Tilly was still leaving drops of blood from where her nails had been scuffed down to the quick. I overheard my human's parents talking about what to do while they cleaned away the fresh blood from the carpet. They were discussing the possibility of bandaging it when the door opened, and my human walked in, slightly browner than when she left. Flo, who had been fast asleep on the porch outside, somehow heard the door open and was in through the lounge and at her feet before I had even registered who it was. She danced about in excitement at her legs until my human reached down and picked her up, where she then proceeded to wash every inch of her face. I was a bit more discreet with my excitement and waited patiently for Flo to be put down on the floor before I rushed over to give my greetings. I was a bit too big to be picked up easily now and so my human knelt down on the floor, so I, too, could shower her with kisses, my feet dancing on her lap as I did so. Tilly, by this point, had registered who was here, and she limped out to the hallway, leaving another trail of blood on the freshly cleaned carpet. I registered the look of concern on my human's face as she saw the way in which Tilly moved to greet her. The desire to move as Flo and I had done was obvious on Tilly's face, and the fondness for our human was as clear as ever. However, her body was evidently failing her fast. She was now a far cry from the dog I had seen knock my human over in her over-exuberant greeting just a year ago.

After a quick talk with her parents, my human went back out and returned a little while later with a small black boot. She gently sat down next to Tilly who was asleep on the carpet, a small blood stain sat soaking on the carpet next to her. She had tried her best to clean it up, but every time she moved, more blood trickled out of her toe. She found the best thing was to lay completely still, which she admitted was a relief as her bones still ached from playing earlier.

As she lay there, I couldn't help but feel overcome with guilt. If I hadn't wanted to play, she wouldn't have joined me, wouldn't have scuffed her nails until they bled, wouldn't have pushed her arthritic legs, and wouldn't be suffering as she is now. I had seen her dragging her leg earlier, and I knew I should have been more careful about how much she did. I knew that she desperately still wanted to be young and denied her body the rest that it needed: and now look what I had done.

As I sat mournfully, I watched as my human carefully bandage the bleeding nails, checking that it wasn't too tight as to cause discomfort. She then put the funny black boot over the top of Tilly's foot and tied it so it wouldn't fall off. The nail was now not only prevented from bleeding out over the carpet, but more importantly, protected against breaking even more. The boot didn't, however, help Tilly's leg, and she still dragged it as she walked, the stiffness from playing earlier making it more evident.

My human, happy with her work for now, walked out of the room to find her parents. Tilly limped over to where I lay and laid herself next to me. She didn't look at me, but instead, looked out through the patio doors and up at the night sky.

"It was my choice to play, Hope, my choice entirely. Don't you go feeling guilty about something I chose to do. Truth is, I don't want to believe I'm old, but my body has different ideas. I think today has proved to me that I really can't do it anymore, despite wanting to. I think I have to admit, as do you and as does our human, that my time is coming to a close. I have had a good show, the best, in fact. I have been very lucky to have had the humans I have, and I know, most importantly, they will not let me suffer. When the time is right, which I fear is not long my friend, I know they will let me go to a happier place where I can bounce along like I used to.

I do have one thing to ask you though, and I think now is the right time. I have known our human for many years now, I have seen her through the good times but also many of the bad times. I have held her when she is sad, and many times been the only one she has turned to. I have sat with her while she has poured her heart out to me, not because she expected any answers, but because she needed to release her emotions, and I was the only one she felt she could turn to. I have spent many years learning to read her inside and out, I have learnt to see through fake smiles, and learnt when the times to comfort her are, and when I can turn the tears of sadness into those of laughter. For 12 years, since the day I entered her life as a puppy, I have been her confidant and her friend, and I fear that the day I have to leave will be the day she needs me most. I, therefore, have to ask you that on that day, you forget everything: if you haven't been fed, you go hungry; if you need the toilet, you hold it, and if you feel sad yourself, you put it to one side. For I need you to be there, as I have these past years. I need you to hold her, to stay there while she screams and shouts and cries, and I need you to stay with her until she falls asleep, as that is the only time she will find relief. I need you to do this day in and day out until the time comes when her pain has eased, and she no longer needs you. There may be random days; weeks, months or even years later that she will need you again, it may be for missing me or it may be for something unrelated. But you are all she has now. Can you promise me you will do this, Hope, for I cannot go until I know she will be safe?"

Every part of me wanted to say no, that I needed Tilly here, too. That I could never replace her. Maybe if I said no, she wouldn't leave us; but I knew this would be cruel. I knew, deep down, if Tilly was saying all this to me, then she was ready, that she had had enough, and her body had won. So I simply replied

"When will I know?"

With this, Tilly gingerly stood up and for the first time turned to look at me.

"You will know."

Before I had a chance to reply, our human walked back into the room and sat herself on the floor where she had been sat before. Tilly gave a subtle nod in my direction before walking over and lying herself down next to her legs. That is where they remained for the rest of the evening, my human's fingers gently stroking down across Tilly's back until they met her failing leg. On the TV, a programme played, but my human's eyes never once looked in its direction; instead, she stared at the plain wall opposite where she sat, as if in a trance. Every now and again, I walked over to try and get her attention, but she merely pushed me away. I could see her eyes were blurry with tears, and every now and again, one would spill out and fall on to her lap below. I could feel the sadness emanate from her, and it was a feeling I had never felt before. I was at a loss for what to, every part of me wanted to clear the tears from her face, in the hope that it would also clear the sadness from her heart. But it was clear that now was not a time that I was needed, and so I curled up on the floor and watched from afar for a sign that I could help in any way. As I watched, I saw a stray tear fall, but this time it fell clear of her lap and on to Tilly's back. On feeling the tear hit her back, Tilly stirred and turned her head back to look at our human. She took one look at the blank face that was lost in thought, tears still brimming her eyes. She pushed her body upright and tried to turn around to face her. Her back leg, stiff from playing with me earlier, struggled to hold her weight, and it took several attempts to right herself. My human, at this point, had shifted her gaze and was now watching the struggle between mind and body, her hand outstretched in an attempt to support the unsteady body. Tilly ignored her own struggle and was clearly more concerned about the mental state of our human. She stepped forward, so their faces were aligned, and slowly, she bent forward and licked the latest tear to escape down the cheek. She then moved her head and placed it on our human's shoulder, pulling her broad chest in until it rested against our human's. I watched as my human wrapped her arms around Tilly's neck, her fingers interlocking across her back. Her eyes closed, and the tears escaping faster and faster until they were falling freely on to the floor below. I could hear my human struggling to catch her breath as she now sobbed into Tilly's neck. Tilly remained steadfast despite her leg now shaking under the strain of the angle at which she stood.

I desperately wanted to go and comfort my human for the pain she felt was hard for me to bear. I stood up and took a step forward, but I heard Flo murmur from the settee behind me. I turned to look at her, but she simply shook her head and said

"Let them be."

I could tell from her face that she, too, felt the pain, but deep down, I knew she was right, and this was a pain that neither I nor she could fix. I curled myself back down on the floor and continued to watch from afar. The pair stayed embraced for a while until Tilly's leg shook so much that the vibrations moved up through her body and were felt by our human. She slowly pulled away, her eyes red and puffy, her skin blotchy with thick tear tracks running down over her cheeks. She led Tilly over to the comfort of her duvet and settled her down. She stroked her head a few times, then stood up, took a deep breath, cleared her throat, and signalled for me and Flo to follow her out of the house and into the car. She spoke no words at all on the way home, and the radio stayed silent. The journey felt longer than usual, and when we finally arrived home, my human remained motionless in the front seat. I placed my paws on the back of the seat and peered into the front. I could see my human sat there, her hands still on the steering wheel, key still in the ignition, staring at the darkness in front of her. After a while, she moved slowly out of the car and around to the boot where we waited patiently for the click of the door. My human remained in a trance-like state as she let us into the house before turning herself upstairs and into bed. The silence was deafening: there was no night-time kiss or cuddle or the usual 'be good' as she closed the door to the hallway. My human was so lost in thought that it was as if Flo and I were no longer there. I settled myself down on to my bed and Flo came and settled down next to me. She seemed to cuddle in closer than usual and she laid her head across my shoulders. No words were spoken between us for we could both feel bad news was around the corner.

In the days that followed, my human remained in a trance-like state. Occasionally, she would stop and pet our heads, but there was no feeling behind it like usual. She spent a lot of time away from home and, unusually, Flo and I were left behind. Whenever she came back, I could smell Tilly upon her clothes, and every part of me longed to see her too. I tried to show my human my desire to come by standing in front of the door or nudging my lead which hung abandoned by the door; but she merely shook her head and said, "Not today, Hope."

She would still take us for our daily walk, but there was no playing like usual. She ignored the sticks we dropped at her feet, even standing on them if they got in the way, and we constantly had to check where she was going as she gave no whistle to indicate a change of direction. At night, she went to bed earlier than usual, and on the nights she did sit in front of the television for a while, the same channel would play, and she would often sit through programmes I knew were of no interest to her.

This new routine lasted about a week, until one day, she came back much earlier than she had been. As I rushed to greet her, I could see her eyes were filled with tears. I could smell Tilly on her clothes, but it was a different smell to usual. Without even saying hello, she walked straight upstairs and disappeared from sight. I remained at the bottom of the steps with Flo as we had never been allowed to follow her up them. From where we sat, I could hear her crying. Despite the sound being muffled, by what I could only presume was a pillow, it was clear she was in a lot of pain. I was torn between rushing up to comfort her and remaining obedient to the rules that were deep-seated in my brain. I laid down, resting my head on the bottom step, and looked up to where I knew my human was hurting: Flo, too, stood next to me, unsure of what to do. As I laid there, I remembered a conversation I had had with Tilly when I was just a puppy. She told me about the time when my human had returned from university un-expectedly. She had fallen out with her friends and was struggling to cope with the stress of the work and being away from home. She had struggled for many weeks until she could take it no more and returned home where the comfort of her bed and her family were waiting. Tilly had watched her go upstairs and heard her sobbing into her pillow, much like she was now. She had the same rule regarding stairs and had vividly remembered sitting at the bottom, torn with the same debate I was having now. Tilly recalled the feeling of longing she had to comfort, that knowing her human was in a state of distress was too much to bear, and slowly, she made her way upstairs. She found her human in one of the many bedrooms; she was curled up on her side, facing the wall that still had remnants of stickers from when she was younger. Tilly told me how she had climbed up on the bed beside her and laid so her body was as close as possible. She then laid her head across our human's neck, so her jowls rested upon her wet cheek. She was afraid she would get in trouble for coming upstairs, but instead, our human turned and wrapped her arms around Tilly's comforting body. Tilly told me how she was pulled in close, and our human sobbed into the back of her neck until she finally fell asleep. Tilly stayed with her until she woke up hours later — she never mentioned the fact she shouldn't have been upstairs.

As I recalled the story and the comfort Tilly had given our human in a time of need, I, too, decided maybe now was a time I needed to disobey a rule. Slowly, I made my way up the stairs, Flo following on behind. There were only four rooms upstairs with one being a bathroom, and so my human was easy to find. She was in the same position that Tilly had described finding her in, her knees pulled up to her chest, crying heavily into a pillow she was hugging. I stood in the doorway for a moment, wondering if I had done the right thing. From here, I could see her back shaking as she cried uncontrollably, and I knew I had to try and console her. I climbed slowly on to the bed and laid just how Tilly had told me to. Flo remained in the doorway, watching to see if I was going to get in trouble. However, my human did just as she had with Tilly, and she turned over and pulled me in close, her arms wrapped tightly around my neck, her head buried deep into the back of my neck. I watched as Flo joined us too, and she curled herself up behind my human's legs, resting her head on them in an attempt to stop the trembling.

I remember laying there wishing with all my might that I could ease my human's pain. I did not need to be told what was wrong, as I could feel her heart was breaking. I laid there quietly as slowly I felt her breaths deepen and the crying ease as she finally fell asleep. Once I was sure she was finally settled, I let myself think back to all the things I had learnt from Tilly. She had been the best friend that anyone could ask for, and she had taught me all I knew. I wished I had been able to say goodbye, to thank her for everything she had done: for all the advice, the words of encouragement, and for teaching me to be as kind and gentle as she was.

I will never forget the feeling of sorrow I felt that night, not only myself but for my human too, who had lost a friend of 12 years. The most loyal friend that she could ever ask for, and I promised myself, while I knew I would never match her, that I would be there for my human as Tilly had been.

Finally, I too fell asleep, knowing that life would never quite be the same again.

EVERYBODY NEEDS HOPE

In the Lake District in memory of Tilly

THINGS ARE CHANGING

After Tilly had gone from my life, I found things very hard, especially to begin with. I found there were many times when I wanted to ask her advice and wished she was still about to tell me what to do. One of the main things I wanted advice for was my human: she completely changed, and it was clear she was consumed with grief. For weeks after, she walked around in a daze and no longer seemed to enjoy the things she used to. Even up at the yard, she was the same: she didn't joke with her friends, or even sit and have tea with them like she used to. She spent a lot of time with Cuba and would brush her until her coat gleamed. Flo and I would always patiently wait nearby, usually, with Flo curled up on the discarded rug. Quite often, I would see my human cry softly as she methodically brushed the dirt away from Cuba's coat, sometimes it would only be a few stray tears, while other times, she would be overcome with grief and end up crying heavily into Cuba's neck. I would watch as every time this happened; Cuba would stop eating the hay she had been happily munching, take a couple of steps back until my human was in front, and then gently lie her head onto her chest. She took long deep breaths, the warm air seeming to flow from her nostrils and encase my human in a blanket of comfort. She, in turn, would bury her face in the long mane falling between Cuba's ears and down her nose. Here, the two would remain until the tears stopped falling, and my human stood back and took one last deep breath before continuing with her jobs. On these occasions, I never even felt the need to intervene as it was obvious Cuba knew exactly what she had to do to help. However, at home, it was a different matter entirely, with many days resulting in my human crying herself to sleep. In these times, I remembered Tilly's last pleading words to me, and no matter how I felt, I always made sure I did all I could to provide comfort. Many times, all it took was for me to curl up beside her; her arms would reach out and pull me in close, and that's how we would stay until I was sure she had slipped off to sleep. However, sometimes my efforts weren't gratefully received, and my human would push me away crying, "You're not her," which I knew was reference to Tilly. The first time this happened, I recoiled to the safety of my bed. From there, I laid and watched as my human cried endlessly into a pillow, unable to find comfort from the grief she was feeling. As I laid there, I found myself thinking about Tilly, and in doing so, remembered a story she had once told me.

It was around the time my human had been struggling at university. Tilly had spent many times with her curled up in an attempt to ease her pain. She had broken the 'no going upstairs' rule on many occasions when my human had needed somebody to comfort her. However, on this occasion, Tilly had known it wasn't going to be as easy as simply lying next to her. My human was not only upset but she was angry. Tilly later found out that a close friend had said some very horrible things about my human and the words had hurt her very deeply. The upset and the anger from the betrayal, along with the struggle of university was too much for my human, and she found herself struggling to cope. Tilly had tried her usual tactic to offer support, but my human had done exactly as she was now and kept pushing Tilly away. However, Tilly had refused to listen and kept forcing her way back. She was pushed away and shouted at until my human, emotionally exhausted, collapsed on the floor — her arms wrapped around Tilly in a tight embrace. Tilly told me how she was unsure if she was doing the right thing by keep going back when my human was quite clearly telling her to go away. However, she remembered a constant urge to proceed: and her instinct had been right.

After remembering this story, the next time my human pushed me away, I was brave, and I did just as Tilly had done all those years ago. I, too, was soon embraced, and it was clear my human had never really meant to push me away in the first place, and the grief had simply been too much for her to cope with.

Over time, my human gradually started crying less and laughing more. She spent more time with her friends, and despite still clearly being sad that Tilly was no longer here, she started to enjoy life again. One person I noticed she started speaking a lot more to at work was the receptionist, Caroline. Initially, they were talking about work-related issues, but it soon led to them becoming firm friends: I also had a big part to play in the development of their friendship.

Caroline had two children: Alfie and Lily. Alfie was the older of the two and was very confident and outgoing. Lily, on the other hand, was a lot more reserved, and Caroline explained to my human that she was currently going through a tough time. She was only nine at the time and was very shy and withdrawn. Caroline had tried to get Lily interested in many different hobbies, but she had never stuck at them very long. When they went out anywhere, Lily would stick to Caroline and not leave her side, which made socialising very hard for both of them. The one thing Lily had shown interest in was animals, and so my human offered for them to come up the yard, so she could ride a horse.

The first time they came up to the yard, I was up there with Flo. It was weird to see Caroline outside of work, and it took me a moment to realise who it was. Once I recognised her, I ran over to say hello and show her where my human was. As I approached, I became aware of Lily who was standing near enough behind her, hidden from view. Caroline greeted me warmly, but Lily refused to let go of her mother's hand; I could see her knuckles had turned white from holding on so tightly.

She followed her mum over to my human who introduced herself along with me and Flo, but Lily didn't respond, in fact, she just seemed to grip her mum's hand even tighter. My human then showed her and Caroline around the yard and introduced them to all the horses and the chickens. Lily didn't say a word the whole time she was up there, but I did notice she let go of her mum's hand towards the end.

The next day, at work, I heard Caroline tell my human how much Lily had enjoyed herself, despite being so shy.

After that, Lily spent more time up at the yard ,and over time, I managed to become friends with her. Initially, she started by reaching down and stroking me, while still holding her mother's hand with her other one. Then, one day, while Alfie was off playing with the other children, I took her my favourite ball and dropped it at her feet. She looked up at her mum for support who told her to go and play with me—and she did! I couldn't believe it to start with, and I made sure I did everything exactly right: I returned the ball directly to her feet, stepped back, and patiently waited for her to throw it, and then repeated the whole thing over and over again despite becoming tired towards the end.

After this, my friendship with Lily went from strength to strength. She would always play with me at the yard, and even left her mum's side to play with me in the field, which was much nicer on my feet than the gravel. We not only played at the yard but even went out on walks together. Again, Lily was nervous to begin with, and despite agreeing to hold my lead, she started off only walking next to Caroline. However, as time went on, I noticed her confidence grow until we would run off together leaving the adults far behind.

We also went to the beach together, and the forest, but my favourite thing to do was lie with her on the couch while my human and Caroline talked in the other room. Some days, I was even left with Lily and Caroline for the day while my human went out. Initially, I wondered why and worried I had done something wrong and would never see my human again. However, my human soon returned, and when I heard her talking to Caroline, I realised it was to help Lily; as it was only with me that she would do things alone.

I also noticed a difference in how Lily was with my human. Whereas at the beginning, she had refused to speak a word, she would now not only talk to her but they often joked and played together. One day, Lily even came to the yard and was left there while Caroline went out. We spent most of the time out on a walk with Lily and I ahead playing and Flo and my human walking behind. When Caroline came to pick Lily up, I heard her say to my human that there was no one else other than her own mum that Lily would be left alone with.

After this, and up to this very day, my human and Caroline spend a lot of time together, with me and Lily off playing on our own. Sometimes I worry about leaving my human out of sight, but I know I am there to help Lily, and so I put my own insecurities to one side.

Since I have known her, Lily has gone from strength to strength. She is more confident in more ways than I can describe. I have heard many stories about how she has changed from the quiet, shy girl she once was; to the active, happy and carefree person she is becoming. My human has told me on many occasions that this is down to me: that I have the same qualities that Tilly had, and without even knowing it, I give people confidence when I am with them. When I heard her say this, I wondered whether Tilly would be proud of what I have achieved with Lily, and I hope every day that she would.

Another major change to my life was the additional family members that appeared over the following year. The main one being the man who came to live with us, which I will admit I was very dubious of to begin with. His name was Brad, and he was a little bit older than my human.

Initially, he didn't live with us, but both Flo and I could tell something was changing when my human started to dress differently and was out a lot more in the evenings. I clearly remember the first time she went out with him, as when she came down the stairs, I struggled to recognise her. Her hair was no longer pulled in to a bun behind her head, but instead, fell down straight past her shoulders. It had a shine to it like I had never seen before and every hair seemed to fall beautifully into place. Her face had makeup on, which I had never seen before, and her clothes looked smarter than usual, and she didn't even sit on the sofa in case she got hairs on her new clothes. Flo and I had to do a double-take to check this wasn't an intruder. A car beeped outside, and she said goodbye, closing the door behind her not returning until the early hours of the morning.

This started happening more and more regularly and neither Flo nor I knew why; until one day, instead of going out, the door opened, and Brad walked in. My first impressions of him were good ones: he made a fuss of us both as soon as he entered and had even brought us a brand-new toy each. As usual, Flo wasn't happy with the one he gave her, so stole mine instead, which I didn't mind as hers was easier to carry around. I had never been one for destroying toys, instead, I liked to carry them safely around and show them off to people whenever they came in. Flo, on the other hand, never seemed satisfied until she had chewed off any attachments, such as eyes and ears, and then proceeded to take out the stuffing until the toy was completely ruined. Ever since I was a puppy and my human noticed I liked to keep my toys whole, she would always ensure Flo never got hold of them. Although there was one time when she was out, Flo took hold of my squeaky rabbit and pulled it apart until the squeaker completely fell out. I had tried asking her not to, in fact, I had pleaded with her, but she said I had plenty and wouldn't miss one. When my human came home, Flo got such a scolding that she never again even looked at one of my toys when my human wasn't around.

After Brad had given us our toys, my human took him into the small kitchen where she had cleaned the table and laid out placemats and cutlery. I remember wondering why she had done this as usually, she would just sit on the sofa, with me and Flo curled up either side. We knew it was rude to look at her when she was eating, but whenever she stood up, there was always some stray pieces of food which had fallen on the cushions, which we were always allowed to hoover up.

This time, though, they remained in the kitchen and ate a meal, which had taken my human a lot longer than usual to prepare. I was torn as to where to sit as the kitchen had an uncomfortable floor, but if I went on the sofa or the bed, I wouldn't have been able to keep an eye on my human. Brad had made a good impression, but there was no way I was about to let a stranger be alone with my human, even if she did seem to be very happy in his company. I decided, in the end, to lie on the rug in front of the sofa as it seemed a good compromise: I was close enough to keep an eye on what was going on in the kitchen, but cushioned from the cold floor below. Flo, on the other hand, seemed content to settle in her usual position on the sofa; saying she would see me get up if anything went wrong. This meant I was left solely in charge of keeping watch, especially as Flo was soon in a deep snooze. I needn't have worried though, as it wasn't long before they both joined us in the lounge, where they sat and then watched a film, sharing a tub of ice cream between them.

After that, Brad spent more and more time at the house with us, until one day, he arrived with many bags and boxes and never left properly again. To start with, both Flo and I found Brad moving in hard to cope with. It felt like we had been pushed out and no longer could we have our human's attention all to ourselves. Flo found the change harder to cope with than me and spent the first few days sulking on the sofa. When I asked her what was wrong, she replied,

"A few years ago, it was just us two. I could run and play without a care in the world. We would go to the beach together and come home and cuddle on the sofa. The only time I had to share her was with Cuba, but I never minded as I could go and chase after rabbits in the field or play by myself until she was ready to go home. Then I got this darn condition and playing became hard: I'm no longer allowed to go to the beach or run like I used to, which was hard enough on its own. Then you came along, and I had to watch as people cooed over you, and I felt like the forgotten, broken toy in the corner. Then I started to feel better, and we became friends, and things got better again; although, I still don't spend anywhere near as much time with her as I used to. Now HE'S moved in, and it feels like I've been cast aside again. It's ok for you—you get to go to the beach together or nice long walks in the evening: but I can't come to those can I? So, I'm left here all alone. Yes, I get a toy or a chew every time you go out, but it's not the same. I know it's not our human's fault that I got this condition, and I know it's for my own good that I stay behind, but Hope, you have no idea how much I would give to be the dog I used to be. This condition has made me sour, and I would give anything, and I mean anything, to change that: I used to be so happy."

And with that, she curled herself up, tucked her nose under her leg, and I knew she didn't want me to respond: but her words hung around my head for hours after. I had never really thought about what she was like before she became ill. I had always assumed she had been the same Flo she was now: a little bit grumpy, with a loyal heart. She had never before spoken about how she used to be or how her condition had made her feel, and I suddenly felt bad for not realising how much it had affected her. I realised I had walked into her life at the very worst time for her, and in those days, that I was a carefree, pain-free puppy; she was not only struggling with the painful headache and backaches, but also with the realisation that her days like that had gone forever. She must have been so jealous of me and all the attention I was receiving, while she suffered in silence. She knew I was there to replace her, and she watched quietly from a distance as I started work and stole all the limelight that used to rightfully be hers. Flo had lost everything when she became ill, and I had walked in and gained everything from her loss: and it had taken me this long to see it. I wanted to jump up on the sofa and apologise for everything, for how I had assumed she was just grumpy, for taking over her life and our human; but Flo, by this point, was fast asleep, and so I kept my apology to myself and hoped one day there would be a time when she would accept it.

As she had with me, Flo put her feelings to one side and accepted Brad in to the family: she even grew to quite like him—as did I. You couldn't not like Brad, he was gentle and kind, and I could tell that he loved us nearly as much as he loved my human. When we were home alone without our human, we would try and make him feel welcome: we cuddled on the sofa together, we greeted him warmly, and I always made sure I brought him a present when he came home from work. However, when our human was home, it was clear Brad felt left out. One day he returned home and placed a small bundle of fur in my human's hands:

"I've got to have another man in the house, and hopefully, he won't ignore me when you're around, unlike these two," he stated, nodding in my and Flo's direction, a sly smirk across his face.

As my human opened her hands to look at the creature that was now mewing profusely, I saw a tiny tabby head poke its head up and look around at what he would soon call home. I listened as Brad explained that he was only 6 weeks old and had to be taken away from his mother, who was wild, in an attempt to stop more uncontrolled breeding.

They sat on the sofa and held him out so Flo and I could say hello. I walked over first, intrigued by the small body, which was making such a loud noise, and leaned forward to try and acquaint myself with his smell. However, as I neared him, he suddenly puffed himself out, reared up on his back legs, and started spitting in my face and hitting me with his sharp claws. I was taken completely by surprise at the ferociousness of the small creature and wasn't able to dodge his attack in time. I felt the needle-sharp claws cut across the edge of my nose as I recoiled back, crying in shock as I did so. Brad and my human both started laughing at the attack: to which I failed to see the funny side. As I slunk away to my bed, where Flo was already hiding, I heard them decide his name should be called 'Chief' as it was clear he was going to be head of the house.

Over the next few days, I kept myself away from Chief whenever he was there. Luckily, when my human wasn't around, he was kept upstairs; my human said it was to keep him safe, which I found odd after he was the one who attacked me. From a distance, I would watch him endlessly chase a piece of string, which hung from a rod in my human's or Brad's hand, or try and catch flies in his tiny paws. Despite never catching one, he was never deterred and clearly tried his hardest every single time. I found myself chuckling at his constant attacks whenever either of the human's toes dared to move under their socks; especially when it resulted in them crying out in pain when his needle-sharp teeth pierced through their skin. Despite his tiny size, he clearly had a large personality, and it didn't take long for him to overcome his fear of us dogs.

I had been lying in my bed watching him play with a small ping pong ball for well over half an hour, when he finally exhausted himself and fell asleep on the rug. I had learnt that when he was awake, he was very busy and playful, he also liked to sleep a lot. It was in these times, that I, too, tended to shut my eyes, safe in the knowledge that he wasn't likely to attack me while he was asleep. However, this time I must have dozed off for longer than usual, and when I awoke, I looked to my side and Chief was no longer asleep on the rug. I looked up at the sofa where Flo was safely positioned (she had learnt that he was too small to jump on the sofa yet). My human was sat watching a television programme and clearly wasn't concerned about the missing kitten. I managed to catch her eye and thumped my tail in acknowledgement: which unknowingly to me was currently being stalked by a small, tabby kitten lurking behind the sofa. I caught a movement out of the corner of my eye, and before I knew it, he had pounced and safely caught my tail between his paws. I remembered the attack from the first night and instinctively jumped to my feet. However, when I looked back at the small bundle, which was now following me in an attempt to re-catch my tail, I noticed his expression was completely different to that first night. Although his pupils were large like before, his expression was no longer one of fear, but complete curiosity and playfulness. I turned myself around to face him and slowly bent down to say hello. This time, instead of hissing and spitting at me, he jumped up and clambered across my nose. While I wasn't exactly keen on being a climbing frame, it was far better than running scared of him, and from that day on, we became firm friends.

The same, on the other hand, can't be said for Flo. Unfortunately, the day Chief arrived, Flo had been playing at the yard in the straw and had slipped down a gap in between the bales. For any other dog, this wouldn't have caused much of an issue, but the slip had pulled her back and aggravated her condition. It wasn't very noticeable in the way she moved, and she certainly wasn't going to let on, but I could tell by her manner that she was in pain. My human had also picked up on her mood, and although she didn't know what had happened, she could tell she was in pain. She always had a stock of painkillers ready for days like this and gave Flo some straight away. However, the flare was bad, worse than I had seen for a while, and Flo remained in pain for quite a few days afterwards; despite the regular painkillers she was taking.

A few days after he had arrived and was now more than confident around me, Chief found out the hard way about Flo's condition. I had tried warning him that she was in pain and wasn't in the mood to play at the moment, but he was young and naïve and thought he could persuade her otherwise. He had the heart and courage of a lion, and part of me was quite jealous of his carefree approach to life. As Flo lay there asleep on the sofa, he took himself to the other side of the room. From here, he had a large run-up, and he took off at full speed across the room. I didn't for one minute think he would make the jump on to the sofa, and so I sat and watched, waiting for him to fail: but that didn't happen. As he took off, I suddenly realised how much he had grown within the last few days, and his feet now just reached the top of the sofa. He threw his claws out into the fabric, stopping him from falling back down. He released himself and thrust himself forward across the cushion: towards the unsuspecting Flo. I jumped up and ran forward to try and stop him, but it was too late. He steadied himself and pounced: right on top of her bad back. She woke with such a shock that her instinct took over, and before she knew what had happened, she snapped out at the unexpected attack, catching Chiefs tiny face with her teeth as she did so. He recoiled back faster than he had approached, crying out in pain; until he fell from the sofa's edge. On landing, he ran into the small gap between the sofa and the floor, where he remained trembling in fear. Flo remained like a statue on the sofa, clearly horrified by what she had just done; to the point she started shaking uncontrollably from head to toe.

When she heard the crying, my human rushed in from the kitchen where she had been sorting her washing. She had only left us alone for 5 minutes, and I could tell by the look on face, she wished she hadn't. She saw Flo shaking on the sofa and started looking around for Chief who was still hidden from her sight. I laid myself down and looked under the sofa to where he was crouched, in an attempt to show my human where he was. She knew instantly what I was doing and joined me on the floor, from where she slowly crept forward until she could just about reach him. When she managed to get him safely out from his hiding place, it was evident he was badly hurt: he had blood trickling down his face, and his right eye was bloodshot; a small blood blister was already protruding from his lower eyelid. My human shot Flo a look that needed no words to accompany it and placed Chief straight into his cat carrier and left the house. After we heard the car pull away, I turned to talk to Flo, but she merely turned her back on me, muttering under her breath that she hadn't meant to. My heart went out to her and every part of me wanted to comfort her in some way. It was as if I could feel the guilt surrounding her, and I wished I could have made it better. I knew it was an accident and Chief was entirely to blame, but I also knew Flo wouldn't have listened to me even if I had told her my thoughts. She was racked with guilt and there was nothing I could do, apart from hope that he was ok.

A little while later, my human returned with Chief, who was much more sheepish than before. He spent the rest of the evening asleep on my human's lap, and I suspected he had been given something at the vets that had made him feel tired. Flo had not moved from the sofa until they returned home; when she heard the car, she slowly slipped down to the floor and skulked across the room to her bed. When my human walked back in through the door, she didn't even raise her head in acknowledgement. However, after settling Chief down, my human walked over to where she laid and placed a loving hand upon her back. She then retrieved a small bag from her pocket, from which she pulled out a small black muzzle. She gently placed it around Flo's nose and fastened behind her ears before giving her a reassuring scratch on the head:

"Better to be safe than sorry for a while."

Flo hung her head in shame at the need to be muzzled, and the look of despair in her eyes was one I will never forget. It was at times like this that I desperately wished I could have told my human what had happened and explained that Flo was not to blame; it was just an unfortunate accident that luckily was not too serious. However, it didn't play out too badly for Flo as my human then pulled out some extra tasty treats and proceeded to feed Flo through the hole of the muzzle. I looked on longingly, for the treats smelt better than any I had tasted before, but my human merely laughed at me and said they were all for Flo, which cheered her up no end.

For the next few days, my human made sure Flo had her muzzle on whenever she was around Chief; and she always got some treats for wearing it. In fact, she soon admitted that she didn't mind wearing it at all. The incident didn't seem to have fazed Chief, and the very next day, he was back to his playful self, much to my tail's dismay. He did, however, keep his distance from Flo for a few days, despite admitting that he had been the one in the wrong in the first place.

After a week had passed and the two had proved to my human they could live amicably together, Flo no longer needed to wear the muzzle. The two had an understanding between them that has remained true to this day: Chief wouldn't annoy Flo, and she would do her best to stay out of his way when he was playing.

Apart from this, life continued on pretty much the same at home. Work, on the other hand, was a different story.

EVERYBODY NEEDS HOPE

Comforting Chief

MAKING A DIFFERENCE

I was now working with some new volunteers from the prison; in fact, many had come and gone since I had first joined as an 8-week-old puppy, and I had not yet met one I didn't like. They had all been great at training me, and it was thanks to them, I had learnt so many tricks.

To start with, I wondered what the purpose of me learning all these tricks was about. I understood the commands were to keep me safe and make life easier for my human, but when I was taught my trick 'Paw', I struggled to see the point in it. However, as usual, I was taught using treats, so it's not like I minded learning them at all. After 'paw', I was taught 'wave', then 'roll over', 'play dead', and 'beg'. I found most of these relatively easy to learn by following the same rules as I had when learning my commands. For most, I followed the treat with my nose until my body did something automatic. For example, when learning 'play dead', I merely followed the treat once I was lying down, until the side of my body touched the floor: and the treat was released! For 'roll over', it was pretty much the same apart from my human helping me initially by helping my body turn until I was laid on my other side. The only ones I didn't do this with was 'paw' and 'wave', and I think I frustrated my human quite a lot when learning 'paw' especially. You see when learning 'paw', most dogs will scratch for the treat that is hidden inside the human's outstretched hand (I only learnt this later on down the line when I watched another dog learning the same trick, and he picked it up much quicker than I did). By doing this, the paw touched the hand, and the treat gets released. However, I had already learnt to follow the treat with my nose and not to get impatient; so when it came to 'paw', I refused to try and get the treat out.

I remember waiting for her hand to move so I could follow it with my nose – but it never did. So then I tried nudging it with my nose, but that didn't work: I repeated this a few times but to no avail. After this, I was becoming a bit frustrated as I wasn't sure what else I could do. I could tell by the tightening of my human' facial muscles that she, too, was becoming frustrated: so I tried again. I couldn't think what else to do apart from touching with my nose, so I tried from all angles: up the top, around the sides, and even underneath; but nothing worked. In the end, my human reached forward and took my paw and placed it on her hand, and as if by magic, her hand opened, and I got to eat the treat. I was unsure that this was definitely allowed, so again I refused to do it until my human once again lifted my paw until it touched her hand. After she had done this a few times, and once again outstretched her arm with the treat enclosed within her fist, I gingerly lifted my own paw and reached it forward towards her hand. I waited to be told off for being impatient, but it never came; instead, her hand opened, and the treat was revealed. Once again, we repeated this over and over until I was sure that I really was allowed to reach forward and ask for the treat with my paw.

From this, I was taught 'wave'. It was one of the easiest tricks I have ever learnt but it seems to go down very well with people and always makes them laugh. All my human did to teach me this was ask for 'paw' but not let me touch her hand — however, I was still rewarded with a treat. I was confused by this to start with but soon started to understand: if the hand was low I was to touch it, if it was up high then I would reach up a few times despite knowing I could never reach.

While I enjoyed learning all these tricks, I still struggled to understand the point behind them: until one day, I had my very first session. The group was at Headway Suffolk and was in a room I had not yet been allowed as it was specifically for the clients' rehab sessions. Around the room sat many clients, some of which I recognised, but some I had never seen before. I was sat in the middle of the group, and I listened as my human spoke all about me; not just my breed and age, but also my beginning and how I was unwanted. For a moment, I started to think back to the farmer, of my brothers and sister, and of course, my mother. I had been so busy of late that I had not thought about them for a while. I felt a small pang when I remembered the good times we had all had as puppies, and I couldn't help but wonder what they were all up to now. I was just thinking of my mother and questioning if she would be proud of me or not, when my attention was snapped back to the room by my human calling my name. She had a few treats in her hand and asked for me to watch her for a next command; I always wondered why she did this as it was obvious I was going to watch her, the treats made sure of that! However, she proceeded to ask for me to watch, and then asked for paw, which I did without a problem. In fact, I had completely forgotten all about the clients sat around watching me, so when my human asked for 'wave' and the room exploded in 'aahs' and 'wows' and 'she's so clever', I was a bit taken aback. However, my human soon reassured me, and before I knew it, I was giving a full rendition of all my tricks. When I finished, all the clients clapped and cheered for me, and as I looked around, I could see huge beaming smiles on all their faces. My human was also very impressed with me, and I found myself wanting to do it all over again. However, instead of doing it again, I was taken around the room to each client individually, where they all told my human what trick they would like to do with me. Once they had decided, my human showed them the hand signal that I understood and together they showed me what I was to do. If I am completely honest, I found this very hard with the first few clients; purely for the fact I was used to watching my human for my commands, and although I had worked with the guys, for some reason this was very different to me. My human was very patient with me though, and to start with, she would do the command alongside the client. They repeated it a couple of times, and then my human tapped the client's hand for me to watch. Alongside the hand signal, my human encouraged the clients to say the trick they wanted too, and the combination made it easier for me to understand what it was they wanted. After a couple of turns, I started to understand, and before long, we were all working perfectly together.

However, halfway around the group, I encountered a gentleman who I found very hard to understand. He had extremely unclear speech and, therefore, evidently found communicating very hard. He had watched all the previous clients talking to me alongside their hand signals, and I think he knew that he was not able to do this. So when my human asked him if he would like to do a trick, he merely shook his head with a sorrowful look upon his face. However, when he looked back at me, I could see a glint in his eye, as if somewhere inside, he was pleading with me. I knew there and then that this was what my purpose was, all these months of learning tricks all boiled down to this moment. I had to find a way to help this man, to let him realise that he was just like anyone else in the room, that his lack of speech didn't make him any less capable or less of a person. I walked forward and touched his hand with my nose in an attempt to get him to show me what it was he wanted, to which the edges of his mouth turned up and the lines on his face subsided: but his hands remained silent. My human at this point seemed to understand what I wanted, and she knelt down beside the gentleman and looked deep into his eyes

"What about if I help you, we can do it together?"

She then put her left hand out in front of his lap and said, "beg," proceeded by her right hand to which she said "wave", nodding at her hands indicating for him to choose. He looked up and stared at her for a moment before shaking his head again. However, it was clear my human was not going to let him not choose. She lifted her hands again and repeated the command options, and slowly he lifted his hand until he touched the one on which she had said 'beg'. I positioned myself so I was sat directly in front of him; but not too close so he couldn't see me. I listened as my human spoke to him about the hand signal, and I waited for the correct cue. As I saw my human lift his hand slightly off of his lap, I rose my front legs off the ground until I was balanced on my back legs. As his hand returned to his lap, I, too, brought my legs back down until all 4 feet were once again on the floor. I walked forward and retrieved my reward from my human who was smiling from ear to ear at what we had achieved. I turned my gaze towards the gentleman and the look of delight upon his face is one I will never forget. As we continued around the room, I managed to sneak glances back at the gentleman, who was still smiling from what he had achieved. For the first time in my life, I knew I had a purpose, and I will admit I was so proud of my human and me for bringing such joy to these clients. I heard my human and the support worker talking after the clients had gone, and they discussed how well the session had gone. I found out a lot of the clients struggled with their speech and communication, although I wouldn't have known this about many of them. She said how it was the most animated and motivated she had seen a lot of them, and it was amazing to see how happy we had made the gentleman in particular. She went on to explain that he really struggled to communicate in many of the activities they do, and consequently, his confidence has really dropped. However, with me, he had been able to communicate just like any of the others, and for once, he was just as able to join in like everyone else. No one knew exactly how the gentleman had felt, but it was clear that they all thought I had done a really good job at making a difference to him, which made me feel even happier than I was already.

After this, I did a few more sessions in the centre with our own clients: each time I came out holding my head a little higher than I went in. I thought, maybe, people would become bored, but they never did. It was clear that some of the clients had memory issues, and for these, every time I saw them, it was like the first time of seeing me. However, even the others, who could remember my name and the sessions before, always seemed to really enjoy spending time with me. Many of them even admitted that when they were with me, it didn't feel like they were even doing rehab.

As well as the tricks, we did other activities together, which included playing fetch (which was my favourite) and grooming. Some of the clients even came and saw me outside of sessions and would groom me, or some would even take me out for a short walk with my human. When we were walking, I had to get used to walking in between the two humans and wearing two leads. My human did this so the client had a lead to hold and was in control, but if for any reason she needed to take over, she had a lead of her own — thankfully, to this day, this has never been needed.

Alongside the sessions, I started being taught a new command, well, I call it a command but it was really just a more difficult game of fetch. To start with, my human started placing the toys down; rather than throwing them. I was then sent out to retrieve them: now I know this sounds easy enough, but without the movement of the toy, I found it hard to know what it was I was meant to be fetching. I mean, I had always been told not to pick things up that were randomly on the floor, and now, Here, my human was changing the rules again. I'm not sure if she knew exactly why I wasn't retrieving anything, but she clearly knew I wasn't understanding fully, and so she retrieved the toy and threw it for me — which of course I retrieved. She did this a couple of times and then placed the toy out like she had originally. This time, I decided to be brave and went and retrieved the toy we had been playing with; it seemed to work as I was rewarded with a treat. Again, this was repeated many times with different toys until I was sure I knew what I was doing — and then my human decided to make it even harder! She started by leaving the toy out, and when I wasn't expecting to be asked, she would tell me to go and fetch it. This, I found quite easy, and to be honest, I quite enjoyed it, especially if the toy was slightly hidden from view. However, once I mastered this, things became really difficult, and I will admit I took a long time to understand.

My human started placing the toy out as usual, but this time, she stretched her arm out to the side of her and pointed clearly to the toy. Now, she had always pointed to show me where the toy was, but this was different, and I knew, instantly, that something was going to happen. After she had done this a few times, either side of her, she then added another toy into the game. One toy was placed to the left of her and one toy to the right. She then stretched one arm out and asked me to go fetch a toy. I remember clearly being very confused as to which toy she might want, and so I just ran forward and brought one to her and hoped it was right. While this technique sometimes worked, and I was rewarded with a treat, it didn't always, and so I knew I had to find a way to work out which one she wanted. I started to see if it was always the first one she placed out, but that didn't work. So then, I tried the last one, then the one that was slightly closer to me, then the one that was closer to my human, but nothing seemed to consistently get me the treat every time. While my human never became frustrated with me, in fact, she was more than patient; the one thing I did notice was she kept moving her outstretched arm. The next time she placed the toys out, I watched carefully, as after they were in position, she stretched out her left arm so it was pointing directly to the pink pig toy that was lying lifeless on the floor. I thought back to all the attempts that had seemingly randomly been a failure or success, and I recalled how it had altered what arm was stretched out. I also thought back to the time I only fetched one toy and the arm on the same side as the toy was always stretched out. I began to wonder if this was the clue I had been looking for, and so I walked towards the pig and brought it back to my human: where I immediately received the treat I had been hoping for. The next time, the toys were placed out I noticed my human's left arm was outstretched again, but this time, it pointed towards the red frisbee, while the pig toy laid on the other side of the room. Part of me wanted to go and retrieve the pig as that had just worked, but I decided to see if my theory was correct. I retrieved the frisbee, and once again, was rewarded with the succulent beef treat. My human repeated this again, but this time it was her right arm pointing to the pig. Again, I followed the direction of her arm, and to my surprise was rewarded for the toy I retrieved. We repeated this exercise over and over, alternating the arms and the toys, but this time, I was rewarded for every toy I brought back. My human's face said it all: I had mastered what she wanted me to do.

I must at this point mention that these tricks did not happen as quickly as it may seem. Some of them took days to learn and the last one took weeks, if not months, until I was sure I definitely understood. The reason it took so long is my human only ever taught me for short periods at a time. Each training session took literally 5-10 minutes before we had a break. I cannot express how grateful I have been for this method, as I always tried my very hardest to understand what it was she wanted. This meant that, sometimes, I became frustrated when I didn't understand, and the break always did me good. I always made sure that I would take an extra five minutes to reflect on what had gone well, and what hadn't; and quite often, it was during my breaks that things seemed to make more sense.

Once I had mastered fetching the exact toy my human wanted, I was then asked to pick up different objects instead of toys. It started with a wooden door stop, then a marker pen, a roll of sticky tape, and even my human's keys. In fact, I'm pretty sure she just found anything and everything to see if there was anything I wouldn't pick up, but of course, I said yes to everything unless I couldn't physically get it in my grip.

To start with, I was unsure about the new tasks as I was always taught not to pick things up off the floor. However, by this stage, I had worked out my human and had learnt when she was setting something up for me to learn with. She would always do the same thing: put her treat bag around her waist, fill it up with tasty treats, and then get whatever toys or objects she was working with in an easy to reach pile. So by this stage, when she placed the wooden doorstop in the middle of the room, I knew, instantly, that I was going to have to do something with it. She pointed and said 'fetch', I hesitated for a moment but then proceeded to collect it and bring it to her. I suppose it was so ingrained in me not to pick items up that as I dropped it at her feet I was still waiting to be told off, but again it never came, and I was swiftly rewarded with a treat. After this, any item that was placed on the floor I retrieved when asked and was always rewarded for my efforts. After I had picked up many various items, my human even went so far as to put paper on the floor for me to retrieve. I found this very difficult to pick up, and in doing so, I managed to stand on it and rip it in half. Immediately, I panicked at what had happened, and I returned the half in my mouth to my human. I expected her to be disappointed at my failing, but instead, she was the complete opposite, and she smiled from ear to ear and kept calling me clever.

I was a bit confused at first, but I watched as she proceeded to laminate fresh sheets of paper, punch holes in the side and tie a ribbon to the edge. She then wrote something on the sheet and again asked me to fetch. The ribbon on the side made this much easier for me to pick up, and the laminate made it much sturdier than the paper alone; and so I delivered it back in one piece this time. I cannot express how happy this seemed to make my human, and she immediately opened the door and gestured for someone to come inside. A couple of seconds later, a client, who I knew well, walked in through the door. She attended Headway Suffolk three days a week, and always made sure she came in to see me. I loved seeing her as she always had time to stroke me and make a fuss, and she often helped join in with my training too. Now this meant she was always giving me treats, which obviously, I liked; but I could tell how happy this made her, which I liked even more than the treats. I cannot say for sure what it was about training me that brought her such joy, but it was clear that it made her feel better about herself in some way. She always left the room with a smile on her face and an extra swing to her walk, and today was no different.

She walked in and sat on one of the seats that lined the walls, and I listened as my human told her about how I could now pick up the laminated sheets. She explained that this meant she could now write words or letters on them, or even draw pictures if she was feeling brave; opening up a whole new side of rehab with me. Suddenly, it all clicked into place, and I realised that once again, there was logic to what my human was teaching me.

After this, things moved pretty quickly. I not only did the sessions at the Headway Suffolk centre, but I started going out and meeting people elsewhere. The main places we went was to care homes, but I will tell you about them in a bit, for now, I want to tell you about a gentleman that started off the visits in the first place.

His name was Rupert, and he had originally applied for a dog to help him with his loneliness. He explained to my human that his wife had died the year before, and only a few months later, he lost his loyal four-legged companion, too. Rupert had had a stroke and attended Headway Suffolk twice a week, but I listened as he told her how lonely he had become since losing his wife and dog. He told her how the hours dragged, and he was often in bed by eight as there was nothing else to do. He felt that, apart from Headway Suffolk, he had nothing to look forward to, except for visits from his friendly neighbour. He spoke in a low and gentle tone, and every now and again, his voice would break as he tried to hold back the tears. He sat slouched in the chair, and his face looked tired and worn, his left arm was contracted and held firmly across his front, and he was completely unable to move it. I walked my way over to where he sat and placed my head upon his lap. From here, I could look up into his eyes, which were glistening with tears. As his right hand reached down to stroke the top of my head, the tears he had been holding back escaped down his face and landed on the tip of my nose. For a while, the room fell silent, as my human sat back and gave Rupert the time he needed. As he sat and methodically stroked my hairs until each one was perfectly in alignment, he seemed lost within his own thoughts. After a while, the tears stopped, and his eyes met my awaiting gaze. In a soft voice that was almost too quiet to hear, he whispered a thank you to me, before looking up to thank my human, too. It was in that moment that I realised my job wasn't merely about tricks and making people laugh, nor was it physical rehab; but sometimes, I would need to help people with their emotional needs, too.

After this, Rupert seemed more relaxed, as if the emotions he had been holding back had finally been released, and he was more able to concentrate on the life ahead of him. He spoke to my human about wanting another dog, and together they went through the positives and the problems they might face. After a lengthy talk, they decided that another dog at this stage in his life might not be the best thing for Rupert—but it was clear my human was definitely going to help. She suggested weekly visits in his own home where Rupert could treat the dog like his own. It would be something that he could look forward to and would be a way for him to enjoy the company without the full responsibility: Rupert thought this was a great idea, and the smile that spread across his face was impossible not to notice.

My human originally trained another dog up to visit Rupert, a laid-back whippet who was also getting on in his years. From what I understand, they got on well for many months until he himself became too ill to visit Rupert anymore. At this point, my human decided not to have another dog, but decided that I was old enough to step into the role. I remember being so nervous on my first visit, unsure of what Rupert would expect from me and how exactly I should behave. I was used to clients visiting me in the centre, but to go to someone's house for the whole day was a different ball game, entirely. However, as soon as I walked through the door, I knew I needn't have worried. Rupert had a bowl of fresh water for me ready on the floor, he had some treats on the side, and a blanket spread across the sofa for when I wanted to sleep. He greeted me with a warm smile and instantly made me feel at home. The hours seemed to whizz by that day: what with bones to chew and listening to my human and Rupert exchange stories, there wasn't exactly time to become bored. Every now and again, I would head over for a cuddle, which Rupert seemed to really enjoy, and a few times, we even had a couple of games of fetch inside. When we left, Rupert thanked my human several times before we managed to get out of the door, and it was clear that once again, I had made a difference to someone's life, which I couldn't help but be proud of.

I continued visiting Rupert weekly for many months, and sometimes, Flo came with us, too. I loved having Flo there, and she seemed to particularly enjoy Rupert's company. My human said she was allowed to come as it was no strain on her condition, and I knew, secretly, she had been looking for something to make Flo feel involved again. On the days that Flo came with us, I made sure I took a step back. I let her sit on Rupert's lap and have all the attention, and I even let her entertain him with games of fetch. I couldn't help but feel proud of her when I saw the joy she brought to him, and it was clear she was over the moon at being at work again. It was a good reminder for me that while I was the one usually lapping up all the fuss and attention, that it should really have been Flo.

After many months of successful visits with Rupert, they then became very sporadic until finally we stopped visiting him all together. I overheard my human and another worker talking, and I found out that Rupert had suffered from another stroke and wouldn't be able to have any visits for a while. As they spoke, I found myself automatically thinking of Flo and how she would feel. Rupert had not only been a great friend to her, but also gave her the chance to feel wanted and needed again. I had no idea how she was going to take the news that we would no longer be able to see him, and to be perfectly honest, I dreaded telling her.

When we got home, I decided that I was going to tell her straight away, but as the words started coming out, she stopped me in my tracks:

"Please don't tell me," She pleaded; a look of desperation in her eyes that I had never seen before.

"Let me just carry on pretending it will all be ok."

I nodded in acknowledgement and watched as she took herself up on to the window where she gazed into the street beyond. I wondered what was going through her mind: was it Rupert? Was it work? Would she feel lonely now or maybe even useless? I decided I wouldn't know the answers today: and neither, probably, would Flo. This was something that we would just have to sit out together, and only time would tell how she would feel.

However, it wasn't long after we stopped visiting Rupert that Flo got the opportunity to feel useful again.

As I mentioned earlier, I started going out to care homes and practising everything I had learnt back at Headway Suffolk. But what I didn't mention is that Flo got to come to some of these, too. My human had to be very careful which ones she could come to, so she didn't overdo it, and there were times when her condition played up and she wasn't able to. But the times she did come were fantastic—not just for her but for all those that we worked with, too. When we were together, my human could ask people who they would like to do the tricks with and would get them to say either our names, or our colour, or our size. She would often talk about our breeds and how it made us different, not only in looks but also in our personalities. We then went through our tricks, and just like I had done at Headway Suffolk, the clients (or residents as they were often called) were then able to have a turn individually. The more visits I did, the easier I found it to understand those that were not able to communicate well, and the times I did get stuck, my human would give me subtle prompts, so the residents didn't notice.

Alongside the tricks, we also played many other games. My human put in to practice the activity where I was sent out to fetch a specific toy. While I knew I only had to follow the direction of the arm, she often made it harder for the residents. She would get them to describe the toy in many different ways; such as the colour, shape, size, or texture. The residents were always amazed at how I brought back the correct one, and I wondered if any of them had worked out that my human simply pointed to it. They also had to aim the toy in a hoop and I was sent to collect it; for me this one was super easy although sometimes a little boring. However, whenever I found it getting tedious, I would watch the residents and how much they were concentrating, and it was clear they didn't find it as easy as I did. They obviously enjoyed doing it though as they would repeat it over and over, and always had a smile on their face as they were doing so.

While I enjoyed my visits and meeting new people, it was clear Flo enjoyed them much more than me. It was as if she became a different dog when she was out—as though she came alive. She would run after the toys with a skip in her step, and she performed her tricks with an energy I could only dream of. Whenever she knew we were on our way to a visit, she would whine impatiently throughout the whole journey, which I will admit got on my nerves at times. However, it was impossible to be mad with Flo when she was so happy: her character came to life, and it was the only time I ever got to see the dog she was before her condition.

I cannot say how many people we have visited over the years as it is too many to count. What I am sure of is that we have given many people something to look forward to—which to me is priceless. I remember hearing one lady tell my human how she used to 'live and breathe' dogs; however, since coming into a home, she has very few encounters with any. She said that she looks forward to our visits, and it is the only thing that reminds her of her younger days.

After each visit, Flo and I will lie together in a way that never happens at any other time. We will talk about the people we have met and the friends we have made over the sessions. We talk about the fun we have had and the smiles we have seen throughout the day, until we finally fall asleep: both of us completely content knowing that we have once again made a difference to their day. It is in those moments, just before I fall asleep, that I believe I am the luckiest dog alive. I look forward to the next day and what might be in store: whether it be a new visit or another trick I will be learning, I really couldn't care- as long as I got to go to work I was happy.

Me and my human at an event for Dementia

GETTING ILL

When I was about two and a half, I ended up needing some time off work when I became very poorly. I can't remember exactly when I started noticing it, but I do remember knowing something wasn't right. It started off with a change to my skin. I noticed when I looked in the mirror it was losing the shine it once had. People had also stopped commenting on how healthy I looked. Then, not long after that, I started to become itchy. It was incessant and drove me up the wall. The only peace I got was when I fell asleep, but even then, I would wake with a burning sensation all over my body. When I say all over my body — I literally mean all over my body — for the most part, I could scratch it with my back leg, and if I couldn't reach with that, I could often turn around and nibble it with my teeth. However, there was one spot on the top of my back that was just out of reach entirely. Sometimes in my haste to scratch, I would end up flinging my head around so hard to try and reach that I would end up doing a full somersault backwards. This often made people around me laugh but it was one thing that I couldn't see the funny side of. At these times, I resorted to running my back along the furniture or a person's foot if they were sitting with their legs crossed at the right height. I know that both of these things irritated my human, and while I was desperate to not annoy her, the need to scratch would outweigh the disapproving look I was sure to get.

With all the scratching I was doing, I started to make my skin flake away, and even made myself red raw in places. My human, despite regular de-fleaing, thought I may have picked them up from somewhere and would spend every evening combing through my hair trying to find one. I looked forward to this time as the comb would scratch my skin as it passed through the hair. However, every now and again, it would catch a sore spot, and I would find myself flinching with the pain.

When days had gone past without finding a flea, my human then turned to different lotions to try and alleviate my itchiness. I had regular showers with different shampoos, and I had various sprays applied and brushed through. However, they were all to no avail. The only thing I found that helped at all was the creams that were applied to the sore broken parts of skin. As soon as they were applied, I felt them soothe the burning feeling, and for a short while at least, they provided some comfort.

After a couple of weeks without any improvement, my human took me to the vets. By now, I had been there a few times; for my ears as a puppy and my yearly vaccination. I knew what was involved, and it wasn't my favourite place to go. The only thing that made it bearable was the lovely staff who always gave me a treat from behind the desk. In fact, with certain staff, my human would discuss what I had been doing at work, and I would often get two!

The waiting room was the busiest I had ever seen it. There was a young cocker spaniel puppy sat opposite me on its human's lap — I guessed it was there for its first vaccination as there were no signs it knew what was about to come. Sat next to them was an older lady with a large wicker carrier. Inside, was a grumpy old black and white cat who didn't seem too impressed with a certain puppy who kept trying to clamber on top of the basket to see in. The lady, who was clearly upset at her companion's distress, moved the carrier on to the floor below; her frail arms struggling under the weight and size to the point where she pretty much dropped the carrier once it was off the seat. The old cat inside growled at the upheaval but then realising it was now free from the curious puppy, laid down; eyes now bearing down on me in case I made the slightest move in its direction.

Sat in a chair in the corner was a very young girl with a small cardboard box in her hands: small holes poked in the top so that whoever was inside could breathe. The girl sat with her mother, who had a loving hand placed on the daughter's leg and gently stroked her thumb forwards and backwards along her trousers. The little girl had not once looked up from the box she was holding, as if it was treasure that may get up and walk away. As she blinked, a little tear fell from her eye. Her hand flew up to wipe it dry as if she didn't want anyone to see. I thought back to the time I had helped Lily get through losing her hamster, and I hoped this little girl had someone to help her if the worst was to happen to her clearly beloved pet.

Lastly, a few seats up from us sat a muzzled mongrel — I recognised him instantly, and a chill went shooting down my spine. He was the same dog that had attacked me when I was younger, although, this time, he had a muzzle that kept his mouth safe behind the mesh. The muzzle itself looked half chewed and the straps had been done so tight they dug into his head. I wondered why this might be: but I didn't wonder for long.

I had only been looking at him long enough to take this in when he saw me looking at him. Instantly, he let out a low growl, and I could see his top lip quiver, revealing the tips of his bright, white teeth. Heeding the warning, I averted my gaze and backed up slowly until I was safely beyond the other side of my human's legs. The mongrel's owner attempted to calm the dog who was still growling in my direction. However, the affection she gave him just heightened his aggression, and he now looked around the room at the animals sat the other side of him. The young puppy (now bored of the cat he couldn't reach) caught the mongrel looking in his direction. Unaware of the meaning of the growls, and before his owners had a chance to stop him, he jumped forward in an attempt to greet the viscous mongrel. He landed awkwardly on his wobbly puppy legs and rolled forward along the floor—pulling the lead from his owner's hand. He ran forward, ignoring the dog that was now clearly very angry at his approach. Before either owner had a chance to react, the mongrel lurched forward, teeth now completely bared at the puppy. He got the puppy within his large paws and threw his head forward snapping his teeth strongly at the puppy's neck. Luckily, the mesh muzzle held fast keeping him safe from the piercing teeth. Traumatised by the sudden attack, the young puppy screamed in fear: the noise from both dogs was deafening and had staff rushing out from rooms I didn't even know existed. The mongrel's owner managed to pull the lead shorter until she could reach the collar, from which she then restrained the dog from making a further attack. Angry at the prevention, the dog continued to rear up and snap and snarl in the puppy's direction, saliva now flying from its mouth making him look completely savage. The puppy, by now, was safely back in its human's arms, still crying from fear. The older lady was crouched over the large basket on the floor, arms outstretched over the top of it in an attempt to guard her precious cat within. The young girl in the corner had thrown herself against her mother's side, who in turn, had placed a reassuring arm around her shoulder. The small box remained tightly held within the girl's tiny grip. The staff quickly but quietly ushered the mongrel and his owner into the nearest room, preventing any further mishaps. Throughout the whole ordeal, my human remained calm and just sat there watching the events unfold. I moved closer until I was touching her leg and felt her confidence move through into my body. It was as if I could tap in to how she felt: if she was happy, so was I; if she was scared, so was I; but most importantly, when she was relaxed, so was I. There had been many times before (way too many to mention) when I had been scared and wanted to run away or hide, but I had felt my human calm and relaxed next to me, and I knew everything would be ok. I don't know whether she knew something I didn't or whether she was better at hiding her fear than I was, but it was something I learnt to depend on.

By now, the puppy had started to quieten down but was still shaking in its human's arms, the girl had moved away from her mother and turned her full attention back onto the little box in her hands, and the older lady was now posting bits of meat through the bars to her beloved inside.

I sat and watched as the puppy was called into the furthest room next, and I heard the distinct cry as the long needle pierced his skin in order to vaccinate against diseases. The older lady was called through next, and only when the waiting room had emptied a bit was the mongrel allowed out and ushered through straight to the door leading outside. After he had safely left, I heard the vet call my name, and I was taken through to the familiar room lined with needles, gloves, and medications. My human gently lifted me on to the table, and the vet examined me from head to toe. As she listened to my heart, she commented on how relaxed I was, and I heard my human state how I was always calm no matter what the situation: I wish she knew I merely reacted to her own calmness.

After I had had a full examination, including a skin scraping from my itchy back, the vet spoke to my human about things I didn't really understand. She then prescribed yet another potion, which she said needed to be sprayed directly onto my coat. On the way home, my human informed me I may have mites, which would be confirmed after the skin scraping, but for now, hopefully, the spray would help alleviate my discomfort. When we got home, I informed Flo what had happened at the vets. She, too, remembered the mongrel well and shuddered at the thought of what might have happened if he wasn't wearing his muzzle. I then informed her about the mites: at this point, she stood up and moved away- she also banned me from going anywhere near her bed. She continually made comments to me throughout the evening, and when I was curled up on the sofa, she refused to sit anywhere near me. It was at this point that I found my heart lurch for Tilly. I knew if she were still here, she would tell me it was just one of those things and would make Flo apologise for being horrid. But she wasn't here, and I knew I would never hear her wise words again, so I merely rolled my eyes at Flo's words then closed them and pretended to go to sleep.

Over the next few days, my human religiously sprayed me as directed on the bottle. I must admit, it wasn't something I was fond of, as the mist would find its way up my nostrils making me sneeze endlessly. My human would try and shield my nose as best as she could, and in return, I stood as still as possible despite the urge to walk away. While I didn't like the spray, I only had to endure it for a few days until the vets phoned my human and told her the skin scraping proved I didn't have mites. They asked my human to monitor my condition, and if I showed any other signs, I was to go back. Flo, at this point, had still been refusing to sit anywhere near me. When she found out I was clear, she stopped looking so horribly at me and started sitting near me again; but she never once apologised for being unfairly mean.

Over the next couple of days, I remained just as itchy as I had before. My human had to apply the creams to my burning skin, which was now even worse than before. I knew that scratching only made it worse, and in places, I had even broken my skin with my nails. However, the desire to scratch was something that I couldn't ignore, and so I paid the price afterwards. After a week had passed, when I was given the all-clear from the vets, I noticed myself feeling not only itchy but poorly, too. When I awoke in the morning, my eyes started sticking together with a thick layer of goo, and even during the day they had a dull appearance. My coat had lost even more shine, and I had a lot less energy. Even Flo had started to notice a difference, and many days she would ask if I was ok. Unsure of exactly how I felt, I would always reply yes, but I could see her look at me with a knowing gaze. After I had been like this for a few days, my human once again took me to see the vet. This time, the waiting room was empty, which I was very glad about after the events of last time. We had only been sat there a couple of minutes before we were called through to see the same lady we saw last time. She spoke to my human for a while, who told her all about how I had been since the last time I came. She did the same examinations as last time, and I could see an uncertain expression cross her face. I listened to her tell my human that she wasn't sure exactly what could be wrong. She believed I had maybe picked up a virus that was making me a bit under the weather. We were sent away with some drops for my eyes and an additive for my food to help boost my immune system.

In the days that followed, I had the drops applied to both my eyes twice a day. If I thought the spray was bad, the drops were a million times worse. Now I don't know if you have ever had something put in your eyes, but my instinctive reaction was to shut my eyes when the bottle came near. I knew it wasn't what my human wanted, and despite wanting to do as she wished, it was something I couldn't help doing. This resulted in my human having to prise my eyes open with her fingers. I understand why she had to do it, but the feeling was one I was keen to forget. Then, when my eyes were forced open, she would put the tip of the bottle in the corner of my eye and squeeze three cold drops in. After the first drop, it was instinct to want to blink, but my eyes were still held open. It was only after all three drops had successfully been put in that I was released and allowed to blink and shake the cold mixture that was now irritating the inside of my eye. If that wasn't bad enough, I then had to go through the whole ordeal again with the other eye. My human always had a tasty treat waiting for me, which made me forget about the experience quite quickly, but come evening, I would have to go through it all again. I did notice that the drops, as horrible as they were, did make my eyes much better than they were before. However, that was the only thing that improved after the vet visit: I was still itchy and sore, and my coat was still dull. The additive to my food was hardly noticeable so I didn't mind taking that. However, it made no difference to how I was feeling, and as the days went on, I continued to feel worse within myself.

After a couple of days had passed, I started to get a strange feeling in my belly. I can't say it was a stomach ache as it wasn't painful, but I found I needed the toilet more frequently. Without going into too much detail, I also started noticing that my movements were becoming much looser than they had been before. My human had obviously noticed this straight away, and I heard her phone the vet for advice. The person at the other end of the phone advised my human to once again keep an eye on me, and if I got worse, I was to go back once again.

That night, after we had been let out as usual, I settled myself down in my bed and went to sleep. However, I awoke after a couple of hours with my stomach gurgling and feeling very peculiar. I was aware it was still the middle of the night as it was pitch black outside and the street lamps had not come on to signal the morning's arrival. I tried to ignore the feeling in my belly, but it became more and more unsettled, until I knew I was going to have to do something. I stood up and tried to wake Flo, who was fast asleep in her bed next to me; however, she just grunted and told me to sort it myself. I went to the back door in the hope that maybe it had been left open—although, I knew deep down, this was not going to be the case. I then made my way back to the closed door that led out to the hallway. I cried for a while in an attempt to wake my human and make her aware of my situation, which was becoming more pressing by the minute. After I had been stood there for a good 15 minutes, my stomach started cramping in the need for me to relieve myself. I knew I had to make a decision: either stay here crying and risk embarrassing myself on my human's floor or make my way over to the back door where I could at least do it on the washable mat—I went for the latter option. As I started walking to the back door, the movement made my cramps even worse and I ended up running in my haste to make it. I made it to the mat just in time, where I am embarrassed to say, I disgraced myself in a very loose manner.

Flo, at this point, woke up and proceeded to tell me how much trouble I was going to be in when my human realised I had messed in the house. I tried to explain that I had tried my hardest not to, but Flo refused to listen. She then went on to tell me that there was no way she was going to get the blame for it. She then turned over and went to sleep, leaving me to spend the rest of the night worrying about what my human was going to say.

I heard the alarm go off just as the sun was starting to rise, and so I sat and listened for the familiar sound of my human coming down the stairs. I remained in my bed as she came through the door and watched as Flo greeted her as I normally would. I felt myself shaking inside at the disappointment I was sure she would feel once she realised what I had done; but on seeing me remain in my bed, a look of concern crossed her face. As she walked over to where I was sat, I saw her nose twitch at the smell that had filled the room overnight, and she glanced over in the direction of the back door. However, rather than investigating the source of the smell, she continued over to my bed and knelt down, placed her hands on my head, and gently rubbed behind my ears. I was sure she must have known what I had done but her reaction was not what either I or Flo had expected, which left me wary still of what might happen next. As she stood up and made her way into the kitchen and towards the back door, I remained in my bed and craned my neck to watch for her reaction. She walked straight towards the mess and then turned around to look at me. I looked about for somewhere to hide but there was nowhere in the small lounge that would suffice, and so I laid down as flat as I could in an attempt to show her how sorry I was. However, she didn't get angry, or even look disappointed: in fact, her face was still one of concern. She busied herself in clearing up the mess and then encouraged me to go outside. As soon as I was outside, I felt the need to go again, and I was upset when it was clear I still had severe diarrhoea.

I wasn't allowed to go to work with my human that day, and I was worried it was because she was embarrassed by me. However, as she left, she assured me I had done nothing wrong, but she was concerned I may make the other dogs ill, too. She did come back every couple of hours to let me go outside, which I was very grateful for. At the end of the day, she collected me and took me back yet again to the vets. The vet could once again find no reason for my deterioration, and this time, told my human to starve me for 24 hours and then only feed me chicken and rice. Now, usually, if I had heard the words 'starve', I would have been distraught. I took after my father in that I, too, love my food; but the way my belly was, I wasn't enjoying my food in the slightest, so wasn't too concerned: I just wanted to feel better.

That night, my human spent the entire evening next to me, stroking behind my ears and across my belly. She could feel my stomach gurgling beneath my skin, and she ran her fingers around in circles in an attempt to soothe my discomfort. While nothing she did really helped, I appreciated her loving touch and snuggled in closer to her support. At one point in the evening, she even heated up a bag and laid it across my belly. The heat was just right and seemed to settle my belly a little bit.

Despite being starved that evening, I still had diarrhoea when I went into the garden. I could tell my human was worried about me, and that night, she brought her duvet down and slept with us on the sofa. She said that this way I would be able to wake her if needed, but there was nothing in my system, which luckily meant I didn't need to. I did, however, spend most of the night in a fair bit of discomfort as my stomach continued to cramp despite having no food to digest.

The next morning, I was still not to have any breakfast, which Flo took great delight in. She even took to picking her biscuits up one by one and walking over to where I was to eat them in front of my face. I tried to not let her get to me, but with feeling ill, my patience was at an all-time low, and so I turned my back and went back to bed. Flo was just about to follow me with another biscuit when my human saw what she was doing and scolded her with firm words. Somehow, Flo thought this was my fault, and she refused to speak to me for the rest of the day — which, to be fair, wasn't such a bad thing. I spent the day at home again — with Flo ignoring me — and by lunchtime, I found I was feeling much better. The stomach cramps had eased, and I didn't feel the constant urge go outside. By the time evening came, I found I was feeling hungry and looked forward to my tea. My human did as the vet had suggested and cooked me my own portion of chicken and rice. Once it was cool enough for me to eat, I tucked in and was surprised at how welcome it was despite being so bland. That evening, my human slept in her own bed as we both thought I was now over the worst of whatever it was - how wrong we were!

A couple of hours into the night, I felt my stomach cramping again, and I had the sudden urge to go to the toilet yet again. Once again, I tried to warn my human who was sleeping soundly upstairs; but it was to no avail. I disgraced myself on the mat as I had done the first night — only this time, it was worse. In fact, I spent the entire night up and down, and in the end, I had messed three times inside the house. Once again, Flo awoke, but this time, even she seemed concerned for me and spent the rest of the night sat up with me until our human came down the following morning. As she opened the door, it was clear she knew I had been unwell again, and once again, let us outside while she cleaned up the mess. This time, however, the mat was past cleaning, and she came in to the garden and disposed of it in the bin, to which I felt extremely ashamed about. However, once again, she was neither disappointed nor angry and seemed to understand that I had had no control over my movements.

The vet was once again contacted, and it was advised that I remain on the bland diet and give it a chance to settle my stomach. However, over the next few days, it did the exact opposite, and I felt more poorly than ever. My stomach constantly cramped throughout the day and night, and the only thing I wanted to do was sleep in an attempt to alleviate the pain. My human took time off work to sit with me during the day, and she left the back door open, so I could run outside whenever I needed. At night, she slept on the sofa, and I discovered that I could wake her when I needed to go outside by nudging her with my nose. After three days with no sign of improvement, I was taken back to the vet. By this point, I had very little energy and it was a struggle to even lift my head, let alone walk. My human lifted me in and out of the car as I was too weak to jump, and she walked at a pace that I could manage. Once inside the vets, the staff were clearly shocked at my deterioration, and they all came over to try and make me feel better. However, I couldn't even face the thought of eating the treats that were offered, which for me was very unusual.

As we sat waiting for our turn to see the vet, a lady with a beautiful black Labrador entered through the door. I lifted my head from where I laid and watched in envy as the light reflected off the dog's healthy coat. The Labrador only had eyes for her human, and I was glad to be left to lie in peace. The owner acknowledged my human, and before long, they started talking about me and the Labrador who I found out was called Penny. My human told the lady all about my problems and how the vets were struggling to find out what was wrong. The lady sat and listened to all my symptoms, occasionally nodding her head in acknowledgement. When my human had brought her up to speed to how I was feeling now, the lady told her Penny had been the same when she was my age. I looked up to see the picture of health that was sat at her feet and struggled to believe that she, too, could have felt like I was feeling now; although, part of me was hopeful that I, too, may soon be feeling better if this lady knew what might be wrong. She spoke to my human about how Penny had gone through similar symptoms, and after a long time, she had managed to diagnose her with food allergies. The lady had found that Penny was allergic to beef and all wheat products and was now fed a diet of duck and rice only. At this point, my heart sunk as I knew my biscuits at home were already duck and rice; and all hope that my condition was caused by my diet was dashed. My human was just starting to explain this to the lady when the door to the vet's room opened and we were called through. My human thanked the lady for her advice, and she, in return, wished that I was soon on the road to recovery, whatever the problem may be.

Once inside, my human relayed everything the lady had just said to the vet, who stood listening to every word. She, too, nodded in acknowledgement at certain parts until my human had relayed all information. The vet stood for a moment and was clearly deep in thought; she then turned her back, bent down to a cupboard, and reappeared a few seconds later with a small book. She flicked through some of the pages before putting the book down so my human could read the words printed. She and the vet discussed many things within the book, but my brain struggled to follow a lot of what was said. I did, however, find out that, as dogs, we have much more sensitive stomachs than people believe. The vet agreed that I could indeed be suffering from food allergies, and it had taken a while for my body to react to the ingredients I have been eating. She explained that although I was already on hypoallergenic food, it didn't necessarily mean that I wasn't allergic to the ingredients: it only meant the food was of a low risk to the majority of dogs. She went on to explain that certain ingredients are of a high risk to dogs: these include some meat products (in particular beef), wheat, gluten, and eggs. The hypoallergenic foods have eliminated these along with other products that dogs are likely to be allergic to. However, after listening to my symptoms, the vet explained that she believed I was actually allergic to rice. It was also likely I would be allergic to the products missing from the hypoallergenic food. She mentioned they could do blood tests, but the best way would be to completely eliminate the suspect foods from my diet for a 12-week period and see if there was any improvement. My human and the vet then went on to talk about what it was best that I was fed, and they decided to replace the rice with potato to start with and go from there.

As we walked out of the surgery, I could tell in the way she held herself that my human was hopeful that we may finally have an answer: I was doubtful, however, that a simple diet change could get me over how I was feeling.

That night, my human cooked fresh potatoes for me along with some of the chicken that was left over from before. She gave me a very small portion, which I was grateful for, as the thought of eating made me feel sick. I remembered the words of the vet, though, and knew I had to give this a try, if not for myself, then for my human who I knew was worrying herself over me.

For the next few days, I had small portions of potato and chicken more regularly than usual throughout the day. Flo was extremely jealous of this and, occasionally, would try and get to my food first, but my human was always there to stop her. This, in turn, caused issues between Flo and me as she would taunt me for being my human's 'favourite' and getting 'special treatment'. For the first few times, I tried to defend myself but, in the end, I let her say her piece while I turned my back and walked away. To begin with, I didn't notice any difference with this new eating regime; my belly still cramped horrendously, and I had diarrhoea, but I was able to hold myself overnight. However, on the third day, I started to feel better; my cramps subsided and my stools became firmer. I still needed the toilet more than I had before, but it was no longer an incessant need. I continued to feel better over the following days, and after about a week of the new diet, I no longer had stomach cramps and my diarrhoea had completely gone. I was still a bit lethargic, and when walking past the mirror in the hallway, I noticed how much weight I had lost. My coat was still dull and itchy, but my eyes had cleared up, and I truly felt like I was on the road to recovery.

After it was clear to my human that I was improving, she spent a long time researching food for me, and she purchased a small bag of a dog food that was made from salmon and potato. She started introducing it slowly, and I could tell that she was as hesitant as I was about trying something new in case it made me worse again. We needn't have worried, though, as the new food clearly suited me. As the levels increased, I started to feel more like my old self. My energy levels went back up, and I found I could run and play just like I used to. I went back to work, and the clients were all so pleased to see me again. I still had a dull look to my coat, but over the following weeks, this picked back up, and it wasn't long until it reflected the light just like Penny's – the dog I had met at the vet's.

After the 12 weeks were up, it was clear that I had made a full recovery, and the new food was the diet for me. The only downside was I was no longer allowed any form of titbit or treats that might upset my stomach. At work, I even had to have my own biscuits as treats, which got taken out of my allowance in the evening meal: although this was quite good as I had put all my weight back on plus a little bit more. Flo thought this was brilliant and anytime she was allowed a treat she took great delight in bragging about it to me. The only thing I was allowed as a treat was a carrot: and luckily for me, there was never a short supply of them at the yard.

Sometimes, even now, when I'm out and about and I see a dog with itchy skin or a dull coat, I wonder what they are being fed. If it's possible, my human will always stop and have a talk with their human about the possibility of a food allergy. Many listen but are often put off by the price of the healthier food; it is times like this that I am forever grateful that I belong to my human, who always puts our needs before her own.

Me and Flo feeling the joys of life

A SHOULDER TO CRY ON

While my time at work was going from strength to strength, and I was now feeling healthier than I ever had before, I couldn't help but notice my human seemed to be low in mood. I can't say for sure exactly when I first saw the change, as ever since Tilly had gone, she had never quite been the same. However, in the months after I had been feeling better, there was definitely a significant change in her general mood. At work, she seemed ok; whenever she was with a client or we were at visits, she would smile and joke and laugh, but as soon as the door closed and we were left alone, I would hear her take a big sigh, and she would slump within herself. It was as if she had been making a conscious effort to hold herself up and the energy from doing so would physically drain her. At home, she would spend a lot of time curled up on the sofa, often asleep; or if she did have the television on, she never seemed to really pay attention to it. However, the place I noticed it most was at the yard: she spent little time talking to the other humans, and she hardly ever took the time to ride Cuba, who was noticeably putting on weight because of it. She did, however, spend lots of time brushing her, or just stood stroking her, while Cuba placed her head gently by her side. Quite often, no matter where she was, I would see tears falling down her cheeks; although, if another human came nearby, she would quickly wipe them away so they didn't see. I would often hear some of her closer friends ask her if she was ok — but she would always say she was fine, and no more would be said. Sometimes, I wished I could speak, to tell them to ask her more, to get her to tell them about the tears she was hiding; but I soon came to realise this was not going to happen.

Flo noticed the change in her, too, and would often lie with her licking away her tears. In the evenings when our human was sleeping on the sofa, we would talk about what might be wrong and how we could help, but we never seemed to find a good enough answer.

Over time, the humans started to realise that everything wasn't as ok as my human implied, and it was strange to see the different ways they treated her. Brad would buy her presents in an attempt to cheer her up; often flowers or chocolates — which always seemed to go down better. Some of her friends called her grumpy and said she was no fun anymore, and one by one, she saw less of them; but some tried their hardest to find out what was wrong. They would come around in the evenings and sit and watch a film, or sometimes, they would convince her to take me and Flo out for a walk — which obviously I preferred; or sometimes, they would sit and ask her to talk to them. Whenever they came around, both Flo and I would greet them and then try our best to leave them alone to talk. I remember thinking at the time that the best thing for my human would be to talk through whatever was making her so sad. I would lie in my bed and watch from a distance and refrain from interfering whenever my human looked in distress. Flo would always lay next to me, which for her was strange, but I think she, too, found it hard to stay back, and together, we could support each other.

From where I laid, I could see many warning signs that my human was upset: she would fiddle with her hands, her legs would fidget, and at times, she even became sweaty and her breathing would become shorter and more rapid. The humans never seemed to pick up on any of these signs, and it was only when she started to cry did they offer any form of contact and support. Lying in my bed watching her struggle and not being able to do anything to help was one of the hardest things I have ever done in my life—and I know Flo felt the same.

One day, it was Caroline who came over in the evening. She had been over many times before, but this time, she seemed to have more purpose about her. There were no films or nibbles, and certainly, no walks. She sat on the sofa and pulled my human in close before she had a chance to show signs of being upset. As Caroline wrapped her arms around her, I couldn't help but notice how tightly she hugged her, every muscle purposefully enveloped my human, and inside the security of her arms, I saw my human finally relax. It was as if the emotions she had kept bottled up inside at last had a chance to escape, and it was a relief to see. I listened as my human started talking, with Caroline, every now and again, acknowledging what had been said. My human spoke about how she missed Tilly, and how she felt like part of her was missing without her there. She also spoke about missing her brother, who was now living in Australia.

Caroline had never met him, but I had: two years ago, when he came over to celebrate their mother's birthday. I remember the day he arrived: my human had been near enough skipping around the house in anticipation. As she waited impatiently, she told me many stories about when they were younger; I'm not sure they were exactly for my benefit, but more to make the time pass quicker while she waited. She explained that she had always been closer to him than her other brother or sister, she wasn't exactly sure why, maybe it was the age difference or maybe it was just because their personalities matched. Either way, they used to spend lots of time together, and with seven years difference between them, he was old enough to take her under his wing. In fact, my human told me that it was her brother that encouraged her to work with animals in the first place. Her dad had tried putting her off as he believed there wasn't any money in animal work, and she would be happier earning more elsewhere. However, her brother knew her better, and told her to follow her dreams as she would be happier working each day doing something she loved rather than earning more and hating her job and looking forward to the weekend. When she told me that, I wondered what would have happened to me if she hadn't followed his advice — I also chuckled at the thought of her working in an office all day: it definitely wasn't her!

She then went on to tell me about the stories he made up for her every night when she was really young. She always wanted him to put her to bed rather than her parents as he always took the time to sit with her until she fell asleep. She had a toy puppet monkey which she called 'Cuddles', who would always be involved in the stories. Her brother would cleverly position his fingers inside, so the monkey looked like it had arms, and at the end of the story, my human would cuddle the monkey while his arms stroked her face until she fell asleep. Only then, would her brother slowly remove his hand, leaving the lifeless Cuddles tucked safely in her grip.

Another favourite memory she had of their time together was camping in the garden when they were younger. They would sit on the top of their climbing frame and wait for dusk, when they would sit and watch the bats come out and fly above their heads. She couldn't recall what they spoke about for the many hours they would sit together but it was clear that the memories brought her great joy.

When I finally got to meet him, it was clear that the physical distance between them had not ruined their closeness. Little things like jokes they shared and the sly smile he would give her were clear for everyone to see, but the subtle ways were just as obvious if you looked hard enough. For many humans, this was never the case, they were too busy talking or doing something to sit back and watch; but as a dog, I had time to sit back and just simply observe. I noticed how her muscles tensed as she held herself back from running forward too eagerly to greet him, how she seemed to hold herself more confidently around him, and how, in return, he looked at her with a proud glimmer in his eyes. When I thought back to the unspoken understanding I had witnessed, I wished I could have relayed it all to Caroline, for it may have helped her understand why my human missed him so. However, as I watched the way she comforted my human, I could see it was not needed, for she already understood.

My human then went on to tell her about the other men she was longing to see again. The first being her grandad who had passed away a few years ago, before either Flo or I had been alive. My human often spoke about him though, and only the evening before Caroline had come around, we had gone to his grave. My human often went there, and she would speak to the headstone as if it was indeed him sat there. The grave was shared with her Nan, but while she always said hello, it was her grandad she always spoke to. She would tell him anything that had happened since she last came to see him, and I would hear her open up to him more than she had anybody that was alive. She would often end up crying and telling him how she wished he was still alive; sometimes she would be nearly begging to see him.

"Just one last time," she would plead.

Quite often, when she became upset, I would step forward and rest my head upon her knee, which was always knelt upon the ground in front of the headstone, so she could face the writing. I think this was so she could just read his name over and over again. Sometimes, she would bring her hand up and run her fingers over the engraved writing, so gently that they would dip down into each individual letter. Why she did this, I will never know, maybe it was because she couldn't read the words through her blurry eyes, or maybe it was because the touch made her feel slightly closer to him. All I know, it was after this that she seemed to need me most; for her hands would become stuck on the headstone. Not literally, obviously, but there was a part of her that never wanted to let go. The first time I witnessed it, she stayed like it for at least 10 minutes before I took it upon myself to do something. Her shoulders had started shaking, and her head had collapsed forward, big heavy tears soaking into the ground below. I was concerned that she was ill for she suddenly looked so weak, as if she didn't have the energy to lift her hand away. I stepped forward and turned so I was facing her with my back towards the headstone. I lowered my head and placed my nose on her cheek, which was cold from the tears creating tracks down to her chin. Her eyes were screwed shut, and she took deep gulping breaths as if she was trying to catch her breath, and she seemed to be completely unaware that I was even there. It was dark at this point (we never seemed to go in the daytime), and the temperature had dropped; I was concerned that if she wasn't ill, she would be soon. So, I turned and gently slotted my nose under her hand and wriggled until I met with her fingertips. Slowly I felt her fingers move, and she brought her hand off the headstone and back towards my head. Behind me, I felt her body shift, and I turned to see her looking at me, a distant look in her eyes—but at least they were open. She started stroking my neck, and gradually, she seemed to come back to life. She leant forward and kissed the cold stone, her grip tightening around my neck as she did so. Then a final push, and she stood up and walked silently back to the car. I followed on behind, wondering how many times I would be needed to help her like that again.

While it had been clear to me early on how much her grandad had meant to her, I never knew why. So when Caroline asked this exact question, I listened intently. My human explained that while she loved her grandad for all the normal things he did, like taking her to the park and having her stay over, etc., it was really the way he made her feel that made him so special. He made her feel wanted and loved and as if she genuinely had a place in his heart. She never felt as though he loved her because he had to, but because he was proud of the person she was. As she spoke, her eyes became distant, as if she was being transported away to a memory that no one else could ever reach. Her eyes filled with tears, but a smile spread across her face like I had never seen before. It was hard to describe, but as if the memory brought back an emotion that she hadn't felt for a long time, and it was clear it was one of both joy and pain all wrapped up in one.

"His eyes would light up when he saw me; he never needed to say anything because I felt it—no words would have matched the look in his eyes—and it is a feeling that no one else has given me."

She didn't say much more after that, instead, she sat staring at nothing; her eyes danced full of light as she looked at the blank wall in front of her. It was as if her memory was coming to light, her eyes projecting it on to the wall for her to watch and re-live. She sat for a moment, Caroline quiet beside her, until at last, she blinked, and the movie faded back into reality. The smile faded with it, and the light left her eyes; Caroline squeezed her hand and encouraged her on.

She spoke next about another man she had known who had made her feel like her grandad used to. She admitted that maybe she was trying to replace the feelings she had felt for her grandad, but either way, she had made a connection so strong she would never forget.

He was a gentleman she had met when she was a carer: before she worked at Headway Suffolk. When she mentioned his name, Flo looked up in acknowledgement, and I realised that she knew exactly who our human was talking about.

While he had dementia and struggled with his brain processes, such as memory, for some reason, he remembered my human. He nicknamed her Knobby because he thought her bun resembled a doorknob on her head. She chuckled as she said it, and again her eyes flickered as the memory crossed through her brain. It was a nickname he had never forgotten, and she ended up being called it not only by him but the majority of the staff team, too. My human explained how the dementia never took his sense of humour, and together, they would tell each other jokes while she undertook his personal care. The dementia did, however, make him aggressive at times, but my human rarely ever encountered this. In fact, many times she was called in to help from other staff members who were finding him hard to calm down. As soon as he saw her, his face would light up, and he would often ask her to save him from the others who were trying to hurt him (which she knew was just the dementia talking). At this point, Flo turned to me and said that she often witnessed our human calming him down—while the other carers would look on in disbelief.

My human told Caroline that after her grandad had passed, it was nice to feel wanted again. I think the fact he had dementia, and while he remembered no one else apart from her, it made the relationship even more special. He, too, would light up whenever he saw her, giving her a feeling of self-worth and belonging that she had been missing since her grandad had died.

She spoke about some stories of her time with him, often laughing as she recalled some of the things he had said. Then she explained how she had seen the job at Headway Suffolk advertised, and she was torn between developing her career and leaving behind someone so special. As she spoke, her voice became quieter, and it was clear the memories were turning to ones that were not so easy to repeat. She explained that she decided to leave, and after the decision had been made, she watched the man she loved so dearly become weaker by the day. The other staff were adamant that it was meant to be: that neither of them would have been able to stay without the other. As she neared the end of her time as a carer, she sat with him while she said her final goodbyes. At this point, his body was so weak he could hardly talk, but as she went to leave, he mustered up the strength to call her name.

"Knobby," he whispered,

She turned back and held his cold hand.

"I love you."

With that, she kissed him on the head before telling him that she loved him too. She turned around to see his son standing in the doorway, a look of appreciation on his face. She left the room knowing it would be the last time and sat with Flo in the hallway outside. Half an hour later, his son appeared and informed her he was now at rest:

"They were the last words on his lips," he told her, followed by a gentle nod and smile.

As she spoke about her last moments with him and the words his son had said, it was clear how much they had meant to my human. Her last shift as a carer ended only a few hours later.

She then went on to tell Caroline how she was gifted some money from his son as a thank you for all she had done. As she talked, she played with the necklace that hung around her neck,

"It went towards this," she explained, "and one day, I want to get a K engraved on it as a reminder of my days I spent as Knobby."

As I laid there listening, I found it hard not to reach out and comfort my human. I so desperately wanted to lick her tears away and distract her hands that were, at this point, fiddling anxiously on her lap. It took all my willpower to stay where I was and just listen to what she was finally saying. I knew this was a first for her: that opening up, sharing memories, and letting someone know exactly how she was feeling, was not something she had ever done before. As hard as it was, I had to give her this time and hope that Caroline would comfort her in the way that I so desperately wanted to. I made sure that the whole time she was talking, I watched her for any time she looked in my direction; she would know that I was there with her, that I wanted to help, but for now, it had to be from a distance.

The next thing my human spoke about was hard for me to hear, but it was evident it was harder for her to say. She stumbled over her words many times and took many pauses while she tried to summon up the strength to say the words that were evidently playing on her mind. At times, I could see her muscles physically tighten as the adrenaline crept through her body, her jaw tightening at the moments that were hardest to say, in an attempt to keep herself from falling apart.

She spoke of a friend, who Flo and I knew very well. She had known her for many years and had gone through many life experiences with her, including university where they had lived together. She used to have a horse up the yard with Cuba, and on many occasions, they would go out for long rides together, leaving me and Flo behind. As she told Caroline about the friendship, I noticed she took hold of a pillow that had been resting by her knee. She gripped the pillow so tight within her fist that her knuckles turned white, and I became concerned what might have happened if the pillow had not have been there. It was as if the emotions she was feeling had come to a head, which she could not contain any longer, and the upset and anger were in desperate need to come out.

I began to worry that the friend my human so dearly loved had become ill, or even worse. However, as my human started to speak again, it was clear this was not the case, but in fact, she had been betrayed in a way she could never forget. She spoke about texts that had spoken about my human in a derogatory way, but there was one that stood out, making me, Flo, and Caroline wince at words. It read:

"Do you think anyone would miss her if she was dead?"

After releasing the words, my human physically collapsed into Caroline's embrace. In a matter of seconds, she had gone from adrenaline fuelled and fit to burst with anger into someone so weak and drained. It was hard for me to watch, and I couldn't believe someone we all knew and trusted, let alone loved, could have been so cruel. What made it worse is my human obviously believed what she had said. She had been betrayed by someone she considered as family, and the words had had a devastating impact. At this point, both Flo and I found it near impossible to remain on our beds. All we wanted to do was run forward and show our human how much she meant to us, that we loved her more than she would ever know, and the words she had heard were nothing but evil.

We listened as Caroline said near enough the exact same thing, but my human dismissed the comforting words that were being spoken. I watched her closely for a glimmer of hope that she was listening to what Caroline had to say—but there was none. As she sat there, I realised she no longer looked weak; instead, she looked cold and distant. Her eyes had glazed over and were now icy and stony, her posture changed so she no longer felt any of the warmth and love from the friend sat next to her. I had never seen this side of my human before, and I struggled to comprehend the reality of what was happening. I kept thinking, 'she will thaw in a minute, she will turn and hug Caroline like she was before'—but it never happened. It was as if admitting what had been said about her made it real, like the words had come to life, and she now had to cope with people not wanting her alive. I listened as Caroline tried to tell her not to listen, but again, there was no response: no twitch of a muscle, no flicker of the eyes; just complete distance and iciness.

Caroline stayed for a while after that, but it was clear there was nothing she could say to help. As she left and closed the door, my human broke down. Neither Flo nor I could hold ourselves back any longer, and we ran forward to try and help our human from the pain she had clearly been hiding. As she pulled me in close and sobbed into my neck, I could feel the warmth returning, and I had a glimmer of hope there was a way my human could be fixed from the words that had broken her.

As the days went on, my human remained low in mood and distant from those around her. She stopped showing any signs of affection or love towards people I knew she was fond of, and it started dawning on me that maybe this was something she would never come back from. It was as if the words had severed part of her heart and prevented her from caring about those she used to. However, the more I watched her, the more I realised this was not the case. There were times when I would see her go to reach out to someone, but something inside stopped her from doing so. It soon became apparent to me that my caring human was still there, but the words rang loudly in her ears, forcing her to remain distant. I didn't know for sure, but I worried that she honestly believed everybody thought the same as what the words had implied. If that was the case, I hoped that the humans would show her otherwise.

After this, a few people found out what had been said and began to realise why my human had been so low in mood. I listened as many told her that the words were cruel and that she should ignore them, but I noticed with every comment, my human became even more withdrawn. Over time, I realised that she was not upset at what she was being told — but by what she wasn't: not one person told her it wasn't true, and that they indeed would miss her. I knew that they were trying to say the right thing, that they wanted to make her feel better, but they were missing the point, and it killed me to know there was nothing I could do. All my human wanted was to know she was wanted; that people loved her, cared for her, and they were glad she was in their life — just like she had felt with her grandad and the man from the care home. I realised that this is why she missed them so much, and the combination of past and present was hard for her to bear.

I soon realised that I could not leave this up to the humans to sort, and so together with Flo, I hatched a plan. From that day on, I put all my energy into making my human feel wanted: I greeted her more enthusiastically, I pined when she left the room, I cuddled her more tightly, and I never once let her cry alone. I didn't care about the 'no upstairs' rule anymore, for if she needed me, I was there within a second. Whenever she doubted how people felt about her, both Flo and I made sure we were right by her side to show her that we needed her. Even Cuba did her bit to help and started neighing at her more and would gallop up the field to greet her.

After a while, it felt that the more we were trying, the less the humans around her were. They became more focused on themselves, and the words that still haunted my human faded into the back of their mind. Part of me was angry at them; I wanted to shake them and make them realise that they were losing her. That the person they once loved was fading into a shadow of who she used to be. The caring human, who once did all she could for others, was now hiding herself away in an attempt to protect herself from the words that had scarred her so much.

While I was angry at the humans, I also understood that they had their own lives. Many of them had children who needed them, and with it, they probably had their own problems to sort through. So Flo and I continued on as we were. Some days, it was tiring, and all I wanted to do was sleep; but I would always hear Tilly's voice in the back of my head and the promise I had made to her.

In the times I laid with my human, I found myself thinking of the dogs and clients I had met at work. I started to realise that how lonely my human was feeling now was how many of the clients felt every day. While my human's friends had struggled to support her as much as she had needed, they were still there. However, for the clients at work, many of their friends had left them totally. I had often heard my human give talks, and she would always say that the clients often lost their families and friends. There were many reasons why — some, because of personality changes; some, because of finance; and some, because of mental health; but whatever the reason, it meant the clients were deserted in a time they needed people the most. I had never really understood the impact of this until now; until I had seen it for myself and witnessed the effect it could have on people. I then realised that how I was helping my human must have been even more important with the dogs that had gone to live with those clients. To suddenly have the love like I felt for my human, to have a cuddle when they needed it, to have someone to talk to again; really was so very important. I knew from that moment on, I must make sure that every dog that came on the scheme understood the importance of what they would be undertaking. That there would be hard times, tiring times, and probably even exhausting times; but if they were willing to accept, then it would be the best thing they would ever do.

Weeks went by, and slowly but surely, I started to see my human improve. She started riding Cuba more, and she took me out for longer walks. She would play with Flo in the garden, and she started to laugh at simple things again. She started talking to her friends more, and slowly, I saw the caring side of her start to show again. The better her mood became, the more her friends wanted to see her and the happier she started to become. As the cloud that had been hanging over her began to lift, I started to believe she may have started to forget the words that had caused it all.

She even ended up getting engaged to Brad, for she realised that out of anyone in her life, he would always be there to support her. While she had struggled to open up to him, deep down, she knew that he loved her, and she now knew exactly how important that was. The first thing she did was take me to tell her grandad the good news. She, of course, filled him in on the bad things, too, but she seemed to be handling it better this time around.

She also received a message from her brother in Australia congratulating her on the engagement. He mentioned how he couldn't believe his little sister was all grown up, and the time spent sitting on the climbing frame looking for bats didn't seem that long ago. I was with her when she received the message, and I watched as she suddenly burst into tears: however, this time, they were tears of joy. That one simple message had shown her that the memories that meant so much to her were also very vivid to him as well.

For a while, I believed that my human was at last finally free from the words that had haunted her for so long. However, there were times when they seemed to echo through her mind once more, and although not as bad, she would once again dip in to moments of self-doubt. She never quite went back to the person she used to be and there were elements of coldness that never used to be there. Part of me hoped that one day they would disappear, but until this very day, they are still evident. I have learnt to accept that while the wound the words left has healed, there will always be a scar that will never completely fade. There will be times when my human will need me; when her friends will not be able to do enough. It is in these times that I will stay strong, no matter how long it takes, no matter how low she gets—for she is my human, and I love her like no one else could even imagine.

EVERYBODY NEEDS HOPE

My human and Tilly

BECOMING A MENTOR

As I grew older, the scheme seemed to be going from strength to strength. My human was able to put all her energy into continuing its growth, and I was now visiting more people and care homes. We also had many dogs coming through the scheme for training, all for different reasons and every one had their own story to tell. While I was amazed at the courage and determination of many of the clients that came to see my human, there was one in particular that really stole my heart.

I was about three and a half when I first met him, and from the very start, I knew I would never forget him. His name was Tony, and he arrived with his friend who was clearly a great pillar of support. As he walked into the room, I noticed straight away that he had trouble walking, and he looked shy and embarrassed. He had two sticks that he held either side of him, and he shuffled on his feet. He walked as if he was many years older than his face clearly showed me he was. He sat down and instantly looked 20 years younger, he placed his sticks behind his chair, and as I walked over to greet him, it was hard to believe it was the same man. He bent down to greet me, and a smile spread across his face like I had seen many times before from other clients. He had a gentle touch, and I sat with my head rested upon his knee while he introduced himself to my human.

I found out he had acquired his brain injury from a car accident the previous year. The accident had not only left him with a brain injury but also other injuries, including a collapsed lung and a fractured back. I listened as he told my human how he could no longer walk without his sticks, and his confidence had been severely knocked, meaning he had no motivation to improve his walking. He had also lost the sight in one of his eyes, which added to his apprehension about walking. As he spoke about the crash and what it had taken from him, I soon realised he didn't just mean about himself. As he started talking again, I noticed how his gaze shifted towards the floor and his touch upon my head became shaky. He stumbled over his words and those he did speak were full of emotion. He spoke about his beloved King Charles Cavalier Spaniel, Harley, who had been travelling with him on the day of the crash. He looked up from the floor and looked at my human, tears escaping his eyes as he did so:

"He didn't survive."

As he said the words, his grip tightened on the scruff of my neck. I felt uncomfortable at the sudden hold, but something told me to remain still, that for some reason, he needed that support within his grip. After only a couple of seconds, he composed himself and let go; returning to stroking me gently like he had been. My human didn't ask any questions about the crash, or of Harley; instead, she redirected the conversation back to Tony and why he was here.

He explained that Harley had been the biggest part of his life prior to his accident. He missed the company and the love of a dog, and he would do anything to have one in his life again. He spoke about how he was lonely and since the accident had become very isolated. He used to be very sociable and would speak to people on his daily walks with Harley, but now he spent his days alone in his house with no one to talk to. At this point, he turned to the man who had so far been sat quietly in the chair next to him,

"Peter, here, has been a great support to me, but he lives over an hour away."

At this point, the man then cleared his throat and spoke to my human. He explained that he was the gentleman who had spoken to her in the first place regarding a dog for Tony. He said how he believed a dog could be just what Tony needed but there were also some concerns he had. He went on to reiterate that Tony was unstable on his feet and had low confidence with walking. He had been given exercises to do by the physio to improve this; however, Tony had been wary of doing them due to his low confidence. Tony, himself, then spoke up about his concerns over walking and a dog potentially pulling him over. There was also the issue of balance, which was required to pick up any faeces that the dog did. I listened while the three of them spoke about the concerns and potential ways to get around them. If I'm completely honest, I switched off a bit at this point and went and laid down in my bed. I must have fallen asleep at some point for I was woken by a very animated Tony: my human had told him she could see no reason why he couldn't have a dog.

As I looked up, the man in front of me looked completely different to the man that walked in only a short while ago. He not only had a large smile spread across his face, but his happiness emanated from every part of his body. He seemed to hold himself taller, and his frame was that of someone much prouder than he was before. He started speaking quickly, as if he couldn't get the words out quick enough; just like a child at Christmas.

"I wish I could take one now, I would have any of these right now if I could," he stated, as he pointed to myself and the other dog that was being trained for its owner. My human chuckled and said that he needed to wait and be patient. Her tone then a bit more serious,

"You also need to be a bit more confident walking before you have one of your own."

Despite the serious tone to her voice, Tony did not look at all perturbed. He was still smiling like the Cheshire cat as he nodded in agreement. He looked at my human and told her he now had motivation to improve himself. For the first time since the accident, he had something to look forward to, a reason to push himself; and I could tell from my human's face she believed him.

After they had said their goodbyes, with the assurance that Tony would concentrate on his walking, my human got straight on the case of looking into what dog might suit him best. Little did Tony know, that only a month later, he would be getting a call to say my human had found him a perfect dog.

I heard my human on the phone to him, but I could not hear what he replied, although, the look on my human's face told me it was one of happiness and excitement. At times, she pulled the phone away from her ear, and I could hear his excited tone muffled through the speaker.

She explained to Tony that she had a 5-year-old cocker spaniel cross that was looking for a home. Her name was Pippa, and from what my human said about her, she sounded very sweet, indeed. The only downside was she would need lots of walking, and I heard the hesitation in my human's voice as she asked Tony how he was getting on with his. She must have been happy with what he replied as she had a smile as she said her goodbyes.

I wondered what had been decided: were they going to get Pippa? Would I get on with her? Would we become friends? Ever since I had met Tony, I knew I would have taken a vested interest in the dog that was trained for him. He came across as so special and in desperate need of a dog that I knew it was important that everything went just right.

I didn't have long to wait to find the answers to my question as it was only a week later when Tony walked back into the office. It was already clear that he had made an improvement since the last time I had seen him. Although he was still walking with two sticks, he seemed more confident in the way he held himself and the way in which he walked in to the office. He sat with a large a smile on his face and as he spoke to my human about the prospect of getting Pippa, the excitement on his face was impossible not to notice. They spoke for a while, and then my human told Tony it was time for them to go. I didn't know where they were going but I guessed from the excitement in Tony's voice it was something to do with Pippa.

It must have been a couple of hours before they returned, and they weren't alone. Tony came into the office first, closely followed by a bouncy black and white Pippa. My human held her lead and followed on behind. Pippa instantly came over to say hello, and I knew, straightaway, she was going to be great fun to have around. After we had introduced ourselves, Pippa went over and spent some time with Tony. I wasn't sure if she knew at this point that he was going to be her new owner, but she clearly liked him, which was great to see. I sat back and let them get to know each other; my human obviously had the same idea and sat back in her chair without saying a word. I watched as Pippa took him different toys from around the room, occasionally stopping to play with them by herself for a little while before sharing. When she became tired, she laid at his feet and rolled on to her back, where he then leant down and stroked her. I could see from the expression on his face that this was uncomfortable for him, but he persevered until he needed to sit back up. At this point, Pippa then became a bit excited and took his hand within her mouth. At this point, I realised how puppy-like she was, despite being a few years older than me. My human made a note of the behaviour, and I knew that it would not be something Pippa would be allowed to continue. After a while, Tony had to leave as he had a long drive home. I heard my human explain that she was being boarded with Janice who also works on the scheme so would get 24/7 training. When she was a bit further on in her training, Tony would come back to see her. In the meantime, he promised he would continue to work on his walking and increase his confidence. He explained he was still finding it hard to walk out alone in case he fell but would try his hardest as he couldn't wait to have Pippa at home with him forever. As he left, his posture changed, and it was evident he didn't want to leave. He gave Pippa a final cuddle before closing the door behind him; I couldn't imagine how he was feeling as he left the dog he had been dreaming of owning.

Pippa settled in at Janice's and showed no real issues, which my human was pleased to hear. She came in every weekday for training and so I got to know her really well. She told me how she used to live with a family of two adults. She loved her humans, but she rarely got to see them. They had owned her since a puppy, and to start with it had been great. In fact, for the first three years, she had wanted for nothing. Her humans had loved her dearly, taken her for puppy training classes where she had learnt some basic commands. They would walk her every day, and at the weekends, she would go for extra-long walks, either through the woods or to the beach. She had a lovely tartan bed that was kept next to the Aga in the kitchen, where she loved to curl up in the evenings or when she was tired after a long walk. She had her best friend Cici, a small Yorkshire Terrier that lived only a few doors away and belonged to her human's best friend. They often went for walks together or would go around each other's houses while their humans spent time together. I could see from Pippa's expression that talking about Cici brought back both happy memories, followed by sad. She spoke about many of the things they would do with each other — her favourite was playing with the ducks at their local park. However, Cici moved away when Pippa was two,

"That was when everything started to go wrong," she explained.

Her usually happy face turned gloomy at this point, and her head hung from her shoulders towards the floor. She stared at the ground for a while before continuing. She told me how her female human became upset after her friend had moved away. She didn't walk her as much and spent a lot of time sat by herself. Pippa had tried, as I had done with my own human, to try and cheer her up; the difference being Pippa's human pushed her away. After this, she seemed to put all her energies into work, meaning she was away from home for longer. When she returned, she was tired, and once again, Pippa would rarely get walked. The male human would at times take her out, but he, too, worked long hours. Whereas before, her female human only used to work a couple of days a week, she was now away for five whole days. Initially, Pippa didn't mind, she hoped that it was only temporary. However, as the days went by, she began to realise that this was how things were going to be from now, and the days started to become long and lonely. Even at the weekend, her humans seemed to have lost their love for long walks, and Pippa never really had the chance to burn off her energy. She told me how the combination of boredom and too much energy played with her mind, and she found herself making up games to pass the time. Some days, she would see how quickly she could empty the bins, occasionally finding something tasty to eat while she was at it. Other days, she would test herself with laps around the house, seeing just how quickly she could make it around the edge of every room, including upstairs where she wasn't really allowed to go. But her favourite game of all was to sit on the chair arm, which sat by the window and see how many people she could make jump by barking when they passed on the path outside.

While Pippa had meant no harm with her games, it had led to her humans being angry with her many times. They always shouted at her when they came back to find the bin contents spread across the floor, often with traces of the tasty treats she had innocently found leading to her bed where she had taken them to eat. Complaints had started flooding in from neighbours and angry mothers whose children had been scared on their way to school. The ornaments that had been knocked over and broken when practising her laps had led to her being banished to her bed and being scolded by her tired and angry humans when they returned home to find the mess. Pippa explained how whenever anything went wrong, she knew she would be in trouble when her humans returned, but the boredom made it impossible for her to remain quiet all day.

She believed that it was due to all this that she had been sent to the kennels for rehoming. She didn't know what was going on at the time and was simply happy to be going out in the car again. She remembered looking out of the window for the entire journey, wondering where they were headed. She started not recognising the scenery and hoped they were going to explore somewhere new. However, when they pulled in to a gravel driveway with the words 'rehoming centre' out the front, she soon realised things were going from bad to worse. She didn't say much more about the kennels for the time being, instead, she started to shake her head slowly side to side and it was evident she regretted everything she had done.

"I didn't mean to be bad, I didn't want my humans to be angry. All I ever wanted to do was to make them happy, but I can't explain just how bored I was, Hope. Every day, nine hours spent alone. No walk beforehand to make sure I was tired, and only a short walk in the evening if I was lucky. I was going crazy. I often needed the toilet, and I knew I wasn't allowed to go inside, so I did anything I could to take my mind off it. I never meant to break anything or to make a mess — please don't think badly of me. I know you would never dream of doing anything like that, and I can see from your face that you are in disbelief I would do such a thing; but please, don't judge me, not until you know what it's like to be that bored. Day in, day out. No radio to listen to, no TV to watch, nothing but silence."

She lifted her head until her eyes met my gaze. I hadn't realised my disgust in her behaviour had shown. I could never have dreamt of doing such things on the few occasions my human had left me: but Pippa was right. I was often tired from work or a nice long walk, and all I ever wanted to do was sleep. The more I thought about it, the more I realised that I, too, probably wouldn't have coped very well if I was left all day without exercise. I told her I believed her, and suddenly my thoughts turned to Tony. Here was Pippa telling me she had been naughty as she was bored and not walked enough, and there was Tony struggling to walk. For the first time since meeting them, I started to dread that things might not go as well as I had first hoped.

However, there wasn't much time for me to fret about Tony and what might happen, as I became a big part in Pippa's training as her mentor, so my human called me. It was quite evident that Pippa knew most of her basic commands. She explained how she had learnt them at puppy training but her humans had not been using many of them and so she had simply forgotten they existed. A couple of them had different hand signals to those she had been used to and so I stepped in to show her what was meant.

There were also a few other activities that I was paired up with her for. My human said these were because she could become over excited and needed to learn to focus purely on her handler. From what I could understand, I was roped in to act as a distraction, but never once was I allowed to actually distract her. Now this was easier said than done, and if I give you a quick run through of the activities, you will think they were really easy. The main one being the circle game. Either Pippa or I was to sit in the middle of the circle and watch our handler. The other one would start out on a big circle and slowly spiral in until they, too, sat next in the middle, side by side, still focusing on their handler.

The other one was the walkway. Here, one dog would have to sit, lie, or stand watching their handler. The other dog would simply have to walk past. Now that sounds easy enough, and for some dogs who were interested enough in their handler or what reward they would get, it was. I found it very easy as I knew my watch command and knew I would always get the tasty treat if I was patient enough. However, Pippa was much more interested in playing. She had a short attention span, and although she was clever and could pick up what was wanted of her, she often became distracted—and that's where I came in.

Whenever we were doing any of the activities, she could concentrate at a certain distance, but as soon as I was close enough, she would try and encourage me to play: this is where it became hard. Pippa had a personality that you couldn't help but love. She would bounce at the end of the lead and desperately try and get my attention. I knew I wasn't allowed to look at her and had to remain totally focused on my handler, but this just seemed to upset her more. Initially, she would bark at me to try and snap me out of it, and knowing I could hear her ended up really upsetting her. After we had finished, she would ask me what she had done wrong, and why didn't I want to play with her. I explained about the training, but to start with, she didn't seem to get it. It was hard knowing I was upsetting and frustrating her, but I knew the bigger picture and importance of her training. It was then that I decided it was the right time to tell her exactly what she was here for.

I sat her down and asked her if she knew why she was here. She told me how she had picked up on certain things, and that she was here to find a new human. She knew she had met Tony, but she hadn't worked out that he was to be her new human. Nor did she seem to know anything about the scheme or what she was being trained for. I wondered how she couldn't have picked up on more. All she had to do was open her ears and listen, and she would have had all the answers she needed. But this was Pippa, everything was too exciting to sit and listen. Most of the time I envied her happy go lucky attitude, but this time, I knew she needed to be serious. Tony's future depended on her understanding the importance of what she was undertaking, I just hoped she was able to fully comprehend what I was about to tell her.

I told her all about Tony; about Harley and the crash and the disabilities he had been left with. I told her about the way he had shuffled into the office on his first meeting and how he had improved by the time he came to meet her. I explained how I had felt when I saw his face light up at the prospect of getting a dog, and how happy it had made me to see him with her on her first day. I could see that she was starting to understand, but it wasn't until I told her about why a dog would mean so much to him that I saw the realisation cross her face. I told her about his loneliness, about his lack of confidence and how he was hoping that a dog would give him some joy in his life again. I told her my concerns about if it didn't work, and I explained why my human was so intent on making her training a success.

The more I said, the more I could see that Pippa understood the significance of the scheme. She suddenly looked serious and the playfulness had gone from her eyes. When I had finished, she looked up at me and asked

"Do you think I am good enough?"

For a moment, I was taken back in time to the moment I had wondered the exact same thing when Tilly had asked me to take care of my human for her. I remembered the importance of her words, and I could remember it was like it was yesterday. I knew that now was the time that I could make a difference to Pippa, like Tilly had to me. I had to choose the right way to make her see, to make enough of an impact, but not scare her. I knew Pippa had it in her to be just what Tony needed, but as her mentor, I needed to make her see it with her own eyes.

"Think back to your old humans," I told her

"Remember how you felt when you were included, when you were wanted and loved. How happy you were when you would do things together. How it made you feel when you would make them laugh, or when you cheered them up if they were sad. Remember what it was like to feel a connection with them, a bond so strong you didn't think it could be broken."

As I spoke, her eyes lit up and danced as the memories flitted across her brain. They were hidden from me — for her eyes only — but it was evident they brought back fond times and the emotions she held were strong. I didn't want to say the next part; I wanted to leave her in this happy place, re-living the happy times she once shared with her humans: but I knew I had to continue. I took a deep breath and pressed on.

"Now, remember what it was like to not have that anymore. Think back to the long, lonely days with no one to speak to or play with. Remember how your boredom led your mind to destruction and how sad you became. When you tried your hardest to get your human's attention, but it was never good enough. Remember how it felt to be cast aside, abandoned by the people you thought would love you forever."

Her face had fallen, just as I knew it would. The sadness she felt was overpowering, and she looked at me and asked why I was being so cruel. What was I hoping to achieve by making her remember those sad times?

"Because, Pippa, I need you to understand exactly how Tony feels. How he once had friends, a social life, people to laugh with and to talk to. He enjoyed life, had things to look forward to, and a reason to get up in the morning. Then, just like you, through no fault of his own, it was all taken away. His friends left him, leaving him lonely and upset. He has no one to talk to daily, and he feels isolated and unloved. You have been given an amazing opportunity, for you are the one that can change his life around. You know how it feels to be lonely, but together, neither one of you will ever feel that way again. You can go for walks together or play all day long. You can listen while he talks to you, and on the days he is upset, you are the one who will be able to cheer him up. You will both meet new friends on your walks, and he will once again feel involved and part of a social network. You will give him a purpose, something to be proud of; and most importantly, a reason to get up in the morning."

As I spoke, I could see the light returning to her eyes. I could see the pictures she was imagining in her brain, and I watched as her tail wagged at the thought. It was plain my words were making a difference: she was starting to truly understand.

"But, for this to be possible, Pippa; you must be mindful when you are with him. You must learn to walk calmly by his side, to wait patiently when every part of your body wants to run forward. Whether it be a cat, a squirrel, or a friend you desperately want to play with—you must, above everything, remain patient and calm by his side. You must put him first at all times. If he is sad, you must comfort him, even if you yourself are tired. You must show him love and affection whenever you see him and make sure he knows how much he means to you. For if you do all of this, Pippa, you will be rewarded in a way I cannot explain. If you think that you can do these things, then you must trust me when I say it will be worth it."

At this point, she looked up at me. She didn't need to say anything for I knew the question that was on her lips.

"Yes, for what it's worth, I think you are more than capable Pippa. You have a heart of gold and a personality that many dogs would dream of. You are bubbly and funny, and I have no doubt that you will bring joy to Tony in the darkest of times. If you can listen to my human and let her show you the way, then you, my friend, will be just what Tony needs and more!!"

As I finished what I had to say, I expected there to be many questions—but they never came. Instead, she laid her head down between her paws and went deep into thought. I left her there to answer her own questions and went and lay by my human's feet. I closed my eyes, and before I knew it, I was in a deep sleep—being a mentor was tiring.

The next day, Pippa came in like a new dog. Any training we did, she put her heart and soul into it. She concentrated on every word my human said, and before long, was making real improvements. My human was clearly impressed by the new attitude, and Pippa revelled in the praise that kept coming her way.

It soon became clear that Pippa wasn't the only one who had been making lots of improvements, but Tony, too. He came down to see Pippa and my human, and to be honest, I didn't recognise him at first. He walked into the office with only one stick. He stood taller, and his strides were bigger and more stable. As he spoke, it was clear that just the prospect of owning Pippa had given him the motivation he had been lacking. He was walking further than he had even dreamt of and was feeling more confident by the day. This became evident when we all took a walk together. To start with, my human held Pippa's lead, but it wasn't long until she handed it over to a very proud Tony. Pippa put all her training into practice, and they walked together perfectly, side by side. She sat at the curbs when asked and remained patient just like I had told her. I couldn't help but feel proud as I watched them walking along ahead of me. I looked up to see a smile across my human's face, and I knew she felt the same too.

After this, things moved pretty quickly. Tony and Pippa continued to improve, and before long, it was time for them to have a trial stay together. Pippa was taken down to Tony's house and was to spend a whole weekend there by herself. It was a long journey and Pippa's possessions took up all the space in the car, which meant I couldn't go. As I wished her luck, I suddenly realised how nervous she looked.

"You'll be fine," I tried to assure her.

She told me how she was worried that she would fail Tony. That she would forget her training at a vital time or something would go wrong, and she wouldn't have me there to guide her. Again, I thought back to Tilly and remembered how lost I felt without her to turn to.

"Follow your instinct, it won't let you down," I told her.

I didn't get a chance to say anything else as my human was now ready to leave. I said a final goodbye and sat and watched as the car drove away. In the hours that passed until my human returned, I thought of all the possible outcomes of the weekend—but not one guess ended up being right.

My human returned and informed me all had gone well while she had been there. We would now have to wait until Monday to see how it had gone. The weekend dragged with my thoughts returning to Pippa at any spare moment. As I awoke Monday morning, I eagerly waited for any news, and it wasn't long until the phone rang. As my human put the phone down, I tried to guess what the outcome was by the look on her face, but she just looked a bit bewildered. She turned to Janice and informed her that Tony wanted to keep Pippa now. He had had such a brilliant weekend with her that he couldn't bring himself to return her. He would be bringing her back to do a handover of ownership, but he would be taking her home again permanently. Instantly, I felt a mixture of emotions: I was so proud of Pippa for proving herself to Tony, for making him happy, and in general, being the dog I always knew she could be. But I was sad at the fact she would be leaving me so quickly. I had become so fond of her bubbly attitude, and I knew she would leave behind a quietness that would be deafening. However, I knew I had to push my feelings to one side, that Tony was the important person here, and he would be gaining what I was losing.

Only a few hours later, Pippa and Tony walked into the office together for the final goodbye. She walked in calmly by his side and sat waiting to be released. I could see her muscles twitching in anticipation to run forward to say hello, but her training held fast, and she waited for the lead to be released. As our humans went through the necessary documentation, we laid together for the last time and spoke about all the fun we had had in our short time. She thanked me for all she had learnt and promised she would never forget me.

As Tony stood up and reached for her lead, we knew this would probably be the last time we would see each other. My heart sank as the lead was attached, and she followed her human to the door. I thought back to the bouncing overgrown puppy that had entered my life only a few months ago, and suddenly, I felt overcome with pride. She had come on so much and was now off to embark on her new life. Just before the door closed, she turned and looked me straight in the eye,

"You were right, you could never have told me how good this would feel," she said before she turned to look up at her human. He returned the gaze, and the love between them was already clear to see. Together, they walked away, side by side, and I knew that this was a partnership I would never forget.

EVERYBODY NEEDS HOPE

Me and Cuba

FAME WITHOUT FORTUNE

As time went on, the scheme continued to grow. I began to notice that people started recognising me, and in my own little way, I started to feel like a celebrity. I began to do more and more publicity for the scheme, and before I knew it, my face was in lots of different media.

It started off with the leaflet which told everybody what we did on the scheme. My human had to change the style from the old one and wanted a new picture on the front. She borrowed a nice camera from someone and off we went. She made sure she had a light background to contrast my black hair against and made me sit perfectly still. I had no idea what this was for at the time, all I knew was I had been told to stay – and so I did.

I sat for what felt like an eternity while she moved around me and took pictures from lots of different angles. At one point, she even laid on the floor, which I must admit did put me off a little bit. After she had finished, she gave me a treat for being so patient. She looked back through the camera but continually shook her head – it was clear she was not happy, and I wondered if I had done anything wrong.

After this, she made me stand, sit, and lay in many different poses while she tried to find the shot she liked the best. She made me hold signs or different pieces of equipment, which again baffled me as to the reason behind it. Finally, she seemed happy, and I was glad that we had finished. It was a few days later when I finally found out what it was all about. A large box appeared, from which my human took out a folded leaflet. She glanced through it before finally turning it around for me to see. The first thing that jumped out at me was the picture in the middle: it was of me, holding a lead proudly in my mouth while I looked straight at where the camera would have been. I couldn't help but think how good I looked and all the time my human took to get the right shot all became worth it.

After this, I had my photo taken for many different occasions and appeared in different media. These include articles for the internet, newspapers, and also magazines. I remember the first time I did a photoshoot, it was very different to the one my human had done, and I remember being apprehensive to start with.

The first I knew about it happening was the fact my human looked a bit smarter than she usually did. Now I'm not saying she went out and got her hair styled or wore any kind of makeup, but she did choose a smarter top. To most people that might sound insignificant, but to a dog, even the smallest changes are the first sign that something is going to happen. Then when we walked in to work, and she tidied the office; I knew that my suspicions were correct, but at this stage, I didn't know what was going on.

I didn't have long to wait though, as before long, two smartly dressed men walked into the room. They were from the local newspaper and were here to do an article all about the scheme. For the most part, they sat and spoke to my human. They asked her lots of questions, and I remember thinking how much her voice changed when she answered them. At times, she sounded shaky and the nerves started showing, but for the most part, I couldn't help but be proud of how professional she sounded.

After they had all they needed to know, it was my turn. I was a bit taken aback as my human hadn't brushed my hair, and I was aware that my collar had a bit of loose stitching, which I hoped they wouldn't notice. My human bent down and placed a 'brainy dogs' bandana around my neck, which thankfully covered the stitching, and I suddenly felt more professional. We walked down to a quiet room where there was lots of equipment I had never seen before. There were large lights, foil shields, and cameras bigger than I had ever seen before. Stood in front of them was a large white screen, which I was placed in front of. My human unclipped my lead and told me to stay. I watched her as she walked behind the smaller of the two men, who at this point, had picked up the large camera and was tightening the straps to secure it to his chest. He popped open a screen on the side and knelt down in front of me. The other man flicked a switch, and suddenly, the lights came to life, creating a shine that made me blink. After a few seconds, my eyes became accustomed to the light, and I saw the man now holding the foil shield so it bounced the light off my coat. The light created a beautiful shine, and for a moment, I became distracted by my own fur. My human signalled for me to watch her again, and before I knew it, the shorter man started snapping away. I performed some tricks, and the man never once stopped taking photos. To start with, I felt amazing, I loved all the attention, and I felt like a model. However, it wasn't long until the flash started to hurt my eyes, and the heat from the light was making me uncomfortably warm. Somehow, my human seemed to sense my discomfort, and she told the men I had had enough. They flicked through their photos and were happy with what they had taken, and so for the time being, my exploits as a model were over.

A few days later, I saw the article in the paper with a large picture of me to draw in the reader's attention. I really felt famous this time, and little did I know that this was just the start.

After this, I appeared in a few different newspaper and magazine articles. Sometimes these were just online, but many were in proper print. After I had appeared in a couple, the novelty ran out, and I no longer became apprehensive. I realised all I had to do was do a few tricks and leave the rest up to the man with the camera. No one ever seemed disappointed in what I did for them, and my human always seemed proud of me when we had finished. I also got used to the lights and the flash until I couldn't even tell you if they were there or not.

What took a little more getting used to though was the filming. I had been used to my human taking videos of me, as she had been doing so since I was a puppy. She had even filmed me working with clients and edited them together to use for advertising the scheme. I even believe she put some on the internet for anybody to watch. However, when I was filmed for the lottery, it was a whole different kettle of fish. Two men came and were loaded with lots of equipment. I had to be placed in a crate when they first arrived as they struggled to fit all their things in the small office. I had no idea what was in most of the bags, but I assumed it was all their photography equipment. To start with, they interviewed my human; I didn't get to see this as they moved to a different room. After this, another lady arrived who I often saw around Headway Suffolk. Beside her walked her dog, who I remembered from training a while ago. I had never really clicked with him as he preferred to keep himself to himself. He was a Shitzu and used to have curly brown and white fur. However, as he walked in, it took a while for me to recognise him; all his fur had been expertly trimmed, and I had to admit how smart he looked. His human had her interview and for some of this he went with her. My human went too; leaving me alone in the now cramped office. I looked around the bags they had left but it was just as I had thought. Large cameras of different types laid neatly inside the main compartments, extensions, and different parts lined the sides. In another bag, there were harnesses that supported the heavy weight of the camera. From what I could see, it looked like they went over the shoulders, but I couldn't be sure. Just as I was about to leave the last bag, something caught my eye. In a corner, there was a small harness with a small camera attached. It was way too small for it to fit any part of a human, and I couldn't work out what on earth it would be for — but I didn't have to wait long to find out.

A few minutes later, the door opened, and one by one all the humans piled back in. They did a quick swap of equipment and then we all went out again, including me this time. We went over to the local park where my human set up some of the activities often used when training me and the others that come on the scheme. She took me through my paces while the men stood and filmed with their extra-large cameras. One of the activities involved lots of cones, and at each one, I had to do a different command, such as sit, down, wait, or even retrieve. The commands were written on each of the cones and would be changed so I never knew what I had to do where. I, therefore, had to watch my human carefully for the correct hand signal to know what I had to do. I really like this activity, and quite often my human would test me to see just how quickly I could complete it. I don't like to brag, but I'd say I was quite good at it. I always had the fastest time compared to the other dogs and didn't usually get things wrong. So when I had to repeat it over and over, I couldn't help but wonder what I was doing wrong. The men continued to film all my attempts, and at times, I'm sure they were trying to put me off. However, after I had gone around a few times, I noticed the men kept checking their footage and shaking their heads—it was at this point, I realised they were the ones making errors, not me; and so, I continued to remain patient until they were happy with what they had.

After me it was the client's dogs turn. He had a simpler course to do as he was not able to retrieve. When I say he wasn't able to, it's not completely true. What I mean is that his owner didn't require him to be taught it on command, and so it wasn't included within the course. I had noticed over the years my human tested us all, but she never made us do anything that was beyond our capabilities, which meant we always enjoyed our learning.

Once we had both gone through the course a few times, I saw one of the men retrieve the funny little harness I had spotted earlier. I was still trying to work out what it was for when he started walking over to me with it in his hand. He said a few words to my human and then slowly bent down and put the contraption over my head. I sat patiently while they lifted my paws through the holes and then slowly they tightened the straps until the harness was securely fastened around my back. I could feel the straps under my elbows, which led from a plastic attachment on my chest up to another attachment on my back. My human asked me to stand, and she slowly walked forward with me following on behind. As I started to walk, I could feel my fur on my side being pulled awkwardly by the straps. The more steps I took, the more uncomfortable it became until I had to disobey my human and try and remove the discomfort. I sat down and scratched behind my elbows, where the straps were positioned; but I only made things worse. The harness slipped, pulling my fur with it, and the plastic top was now sat awkwardly against my side. My human corrected it, but my fur was still pulling, and I couldn't help but stop and try to sort it again. I hated being disobedient, but the feeling was not only uncomfortable but also distracting. I knew, soon, I would be asked to do something, and unless I could give my human my full concentration, I knew I wouldn't do the best job possible. However, this time when I sat down, my human walked back to me,

"What's up?" She asked me.

I wished I could tell her, but it appeared I didn't need to. She carefully released the straps and smoothed out the fur from underneath. As she tightened them back up, she checked that nothing was caught again. She then walked away; this time, there was no pulling at all, and I was able to follow on comfortably behind. I could feel the straps under my elbows and the plastic on my chest and back, but it didn't take long for me to pretty much forget about them. I was still unsure what the harness was for when the man walked back over to me with two very small cameras. He attached one to the plastic strapped to my chest and one to my back. My human then took me for another little walk to check I was happy with them, which I was; in fact, I could hardly feel them they were so small. With the cameras securely in place, we then went on to play the 'find it game'. This was my favourite game of all—especially when Flo was there. We often played it in care homes as the residents really seemed to enjoy it. Basically, the idea was that my human would make us wait out of sight while she hid a specific toy that was filled with tasty treats—we would then find it. Sometimes it was quite easy, and we could see it, but more often than not, it was hidden out of sight, so we had to rely totally on our noses. When we first used to play, Flo always used to find it really easily, which always impressed my human. In fact, she used to run straight to where it was, which always puzzled me as I would take a while to find it. To start with, I tried harder and really strained to block out everything else and concentrate only on my nose and isolating where the scent was strongest. While I improved, I was still nowhere near as good as Flo, and I just couldn't work out why;

until I watched her closely one day. My human had told us to wait where she always did; it was a small annexe off from the main room where the residents were all sat. As she walked away to hide the toy, I saw Flo change her position and crane her neck around the edge of the wall before returning back to her place. Two seconds later, my human returned and asked her to go find the toy; not surprisingly, she ran straight to where it was. Suddenly it all became clear — she had been watching where the toy was hidden all this time. The more I thought about it, the more I remembered little things that now made sense: she always made sure she sat close to the edge of the wall, she always wanted to go first, and she always crept forward if asked to sit further back. I had to laugh when I realised what she had been doing, she was far cleverer than I ever gave her credit for. It wasn't long before my human also realised what was happening though. I think she must have seen Flo cheating as she came back very quickly, the toy still in her hand, and moved Flo back so she was even further back behind me. From this point on, Flo never managed to find it straight away and had to rely on her nose, too. This meant that, for a while, I was better than her, which I must admit felt great.

However, today was very different: no residents, no care home, no Flo, and for the first time, I was asked to do it outside. The men no longer filmed, and I assumed they must have been getting the footage from the cameras attached to my harness. We walked over to the side of the field where there was an area of different terrain. There was a natural crater lined with bushes and little paths leading through to the other side. My human made me wait on the field while she walked down into the crater and out of my sight. She appeared a little while later, minus the toy, and asked me to go find it. As I ran forward to the edge of the crater, I knew this was going to be harder than normal. There were many more smells in the air, all mixing together, and already, I was struggling to track where my human had gone. I put my nose to the floor and tried to block out all other scents. I ran into a couple of bushes but to no avail; then on the third pass, I caught a faint scent that I recognised. I went in and followed the direction of the scent until it became stronger. Then it went weaker, and I knew I must have passed it. I doubled back on myself, slowed myself up, and went from side to side until the scent was so strong, I knew I was close: and then I saw it. Tucked in between the twigs and the leaves of a bush, barely visible, was the toy I had been searching for. Relieved I had managed it; I delicately retrieved it and ran proudly back to my human. As I appeared over the edge of the crater, my human threw her arms up in the air in delight at my success, the two men burst into applause by her side. As I dropped the toy at her feet and received my reward, I felt overwhelmed with pride.

As they took the harness off and we finished for the day, I felt a mixture of emotions. I was tired and relieved it was over, but at the same time, happy and proud. I had managed to show the men how well I could do the activities, and it was clear by their faces they were impressed. My human was also very proud of me, which to me, meant more than anything else. I couldn't wait to see the final piece once all the footage had been put together. It came out a little while later, and all our hard work had paid off. It showed everything that the scheme achieves, and although a lot of what I had done on the day wasn't displayed, I was still pleased that I had been a part of it all.

While the filming was harder than the photos because you had little room for error, at least there was always the chance to try again. The filming could be cut and edited if something didn't go quite right, which was far from the case when I had to go to live events.

There were many different events I attended, all for different purposes. Some involved raising awareness about something in particular, such as dementia, while some were to inform people more about the work we do. I have been to so many over the years that to recall them all would be ludicrous; however, I will take you through some of the ones I remember well.

The first event I ever did was to raise awareness of mental health issues. I remember it clearly as I was still very young when I went. It was very small and so my human thought it would give me good exposure without overwhelming me. It was set up in a large hall, not far from the office. As we walked in, there were tables lining both sides. People were busily preparing stands and signs and arranging different items on their tables. It was hard to tell what was going on to start with, and I was a little apprehensive. We stopped by a table which had 'Headway Suffolk' written on a small sign in the middle, and my human gave me a treat and stood with me while her colleague busied herself preparing the empty table. A few people noticed me and paused to say hello, but quickly carried on with what they were doing. After a while, I noticed the activity start to die down, and people took their places behind the tables. I took the time to look around at all the organisations and the displays that were now fully set up. There were some I had heard staff at Headway talking about before, but there were many I had never seen or heard of before. They all had leaflets explaining what they did, and many had free handouts, such as pens or keyrings. As I looked at our display, I noticed we didn't have anything to draw people over to the table, and I wondered how we would compete with the other tables.

As the doors opened and the public started coming in, the activity levels picked up very quickly. They made their way around the tables and stopped and talked to the staff standing patiently behind each one. It wasn't long until I was spotted, and after that, it was non-stop. I had many people come and say hello to me, and while I only knew a couple of tricks at that age, I performed them as well as I could. I didn't have much time to rest to begin with, and I soon realised we didn't need keyrings or pens to draw people over, as it appeared I was the star attraction. To be honest, though, I loved all the attention. I felt very special, and everybody that met me was very kind and gentle. My human was just as busy as me, and she spoke to everybody that came to say hello. She spoke about the scheme and what my job role was, and then she went on to talk about Headway in general.

In the afternoon, the atmosphere changed, and the stalls were much quieter. A few productions went on up the top end of the room, which everybody stopped to watch. I took this opportunity to lie down and have a rest. The morning had taken its toll on me, and I suddenly felt very tired. As I laid there, I learnt I could block out the sounds and activities around me. Every now and again, something would wake me from my slumber, but for the most part, I felt content enough to sleep. After a while, I woke to see a lady talking to my human; she looked down at me as she spoke,

"Not many dogs would be relaxed enough to sleep with all this going on, especially not as young as her- you've got a good one there."

She nodded in my direction and walked away, turning to look back to where I still laid half asleep. I thought about her words; was it unusual? Was it good that I could sleep amongst the activity? Would other dogs really not have done the same thing if they were tired? All I knew was I felt safe with my human the other side of my lead, knowing that she would wake me if needed. I looked up to see her watching me, a proud smile across her face, and I knew she was pleased with me, and to me, that was all that mattered.

At the end of the day, my human and her colleague cleared away the stand. I said goodbye to the other stall holders that came over and had my last bits of attention for the day. We had spoken to lots of people, ranging from other organisations through to potential clients, and the day had been a total success. As we walked back to the car, my human told me how I was a 'star' and had 'done her proud'. I wasn't exactly sure what I had done apart from meet and greet people, but I was pleased to hear she was happy with me. To be perfectly honest, I had really enjoyed myself, I had met lots of people and had enjoyed all the activity that the day had brought. I found myself looking forward to another event and hoped that I would be allowed to attend.

I needn't have worried, for as I've already mentioned, I was allowed to attend many more events after that day, some of which were considerably larger. The biggest one I can remember attending was the county show on which we had a stall. It was a very early start, and we had bags of equipment with us. It had been raining very heavily in the days leading up to the event, and consequently, the ground was water-logged. My human had to park quite a way from the showground, as she was worried her car would get stuck in the soft soil. She had a colleague with her, and together, they unpacked the car with all their equipment. They had a table, bags of leaflets, a bed and bowl for me, a toy game for the children to play with, and a large toy dog as a prize. As they picked up all the equipment between them, I suddenly realised just how much they had. My human only had a spare little finger on which she hooked my lead, and together, we made our way to the showground. The walk took a lot longer than it should have with my human and her colleague needing to stop to rearrange carrying techniques many times along the way. As we finally approached the entrance to the showground, I caught the strong scent of rabbits that lived in the large hedgerows around the perimeter. My instinct was strong, and every part of me wanted to put my nose to the floor. The rain had brought the smells to life and they were stronger than I had ever experienced before. However, I was aware of the heavy load my human was now puffing and panting under the strain of, and I knew the slightest test of balance might send them all tumbling to the floor. I gently tested to see if there was enough slack in the lead, but just inches from the ground I felt my collar tighten, and I knew any more would pull the lead that was precariously balanced around my human's finger. For the rest of the walk, my willpower was tested to its limit. I knew I shouldn't pull down to smell, but the scents were hitting my nose enticing me to give in to them. I tried to block them out by watching everyone else arriving at the showground, either by car or walking like us. Those that had dared to drive were mainly in cars much larger than the ones my human drove and seemed to handle the ground ok; but a couple of smaller ones struggled, and I knew my human had made the right decision to walk, despite the added effort it had entailed. As we walked across the showground, we started to hit a hive of activity. It was split up into aisles of large gazebos, some of which were still closed up, but many were well underway with setting up. We walked halfway up the lines of stalls until we stopped outside one which had not yet been opened. My human and her colleague set about opening it and arranging the equipment they had brought with them. Before long, they had made it their own, and the stall was ready for whatever the day might entail. At this point, I had no idea about what the show would bring, or indeed, the vast amount of people that would attend: but it wasn't long until I found out.

The public started arriving in small numbers, but within an hour, there were more people than I had ever seen in one place. Many walked past the stall without giving us much attention, but some stopped to say hello. Just like at the other events, my human told them about Headway Suffolk in general, and then spoke about the scheme in particular. At this point in my life, I knew a few more tricks and was asked to show those who were interested what I knew. I found that once I started, more people came over to see me, and before I knew it, I was in front of a small crowd. After I had finished, my human asked if anybody else would like to do any tricks with me, which always went down well—especially with the children. After this, many people would put a small donation in the box or the children would have a go at the game to try and win the toy dog, which looked quite a lot like me.

As the day went on, more and more people came over to see us, and I even heard people say,

"Here's the dog they were talking about."

Every now and again, the attention would drop off, and I would sneak on to my bed at the back of the stall for a quick nap. I sometimes awoke to hear my human explain I was on a well-deserved break, but more often than not, I would get up to go and say hello.

About halfway through the day, my human took me for a walk away from the stall, so I could have a toilet break and a stretch of the legs. We walked away from the rows of stalls and entered even more hive of activity. There were large rings around which people stood and watched the events going on inside. Some had horses or cows parading around, while others had displays going on inside the ring. There were large tractors stood shining in the sun and sheep being herded up by collies. Everywhere I looked, there was something different going on, and I couldn't help but feel alive in the atmosphere. Walking around the rings were a mass of adults, children, and dogs, all going in different directions. Some were rushing to a watch a particular ring, while others seemed happy to mooch in and out of the stalls, many carrying large bags containing the bargains they had managed to buy. We sat on a seat at the quieter end of the showground, and my human had her lunch. She sat and watched a pair of beautiful grey horses pulling a stunning carriage behind them. As they trotted elegantly around the outside of the ring, you couldn't help but become entranced by their movement and grace. They seemed to float across the surface, despite the carriage leaving large furrows where the wheels struggled on the soft ground. They had large feathers, which stood up from their immaculate manes, and the sun bounced off their finely groomed coats. We had only been watching them for what felt like five minutes before my human stood again, and we headed back towards our stall.

On the way back, we became stuck in a crowd of people gathering around the food tents. As my human tried to find a way through, I couldn't help but notice a small terrier that was stood outside another stall. Its humans were stood with their back to him while they debated over what size jacket to buy their small child who was clearly much more interested in the tractors over the other side of the walkway. The terrier was eye-balling a small mongrel, which was stood outside the stall next to him; his humans, too, were distracted by the items inside the stall. As they sidled their way along the contents of the stall, they made their way closer to the terrier, who by this point, was getting rather anxious about the proximity of the mongrel. A couple more steps over, and the mongrel was within touching distance of the terrier. Both sets of humans were completely unaware of their dogs, and the mongrel missed the warning signals that the terrier was giving off. He stepped forward to say hello, but the terrier feeling threatened lurched forward, catching the mongrel off-guard. The two fell to the floor in a scuffle of snapping and snarling, entangling their leads as they did so. Only then did the owners take note of what was going on behind them, and they tried in vain to get their dogs under control. Everybody around stopped to watch the two dogs who were now tearing chunks of fur from each other; their owners screaming at them to stop. Children broke out in tears, worried for the dog's safety, and their parents tried ushering them away from the scene. A large burly man, dressed in jeans, wellington boots, a chequered shirt, and tweed hat ran across the walkway from where he had been displaying his vintage tractor. In one swoop, he reached down and scruffed each dog in either hand, pulling them apart as he did so. As they squirmed within his grasp, shocked at the sudden interruption, it was clear that neither was seriously hurt. He thrust them into their human's chests before turning tail and heading back to his tractor, muttering under his breath as he did so. The humans apologised to each other and headed off in different directions, and we finally managed to make our way back to our stall.

We hadn't long been back at the stall when I saw the terrier appear down our aisle. His humans hadn't seemed to learn from the events of earlier as the terrier strained at the end of the leash, once again, doing its own thing without them paying him the slightest bit of attention. As they neared the stall, my human, too, caught sight of the terrier and summoned for me to back up slightly behind her. The young boy ran over to the stall and picked up the toy dog,

"Mummy I want this one," he shouted over to his mother, who was once again distracted by something on the next stall. Without even looking up, she handed him the money needed to enter, and he wandered over to have a go on the game. His parents remained on the stall next to us, and the terrier suddenly spotted me. He darted behind his human's legs and dived over to where I was sat minding my own business. My human had obviously kept an eye on the troublesome terrier, and before I knew it, had put her foot in front of me blocking its way. Safe behind my human's legs I let out a sigh of relief and waited until the terrier had been dragged away by his careless owners. My human shook her head in dismay as they walked away, leaning down to rub my head as she did so.

The rest of the day, despite being busy, went without a hitch. As time went by, the crowds started to die down, and I managed to get more rest. I laid and watched people pass by, many now looking worn out from their hours traipsing around the showground. The few children that still remained were irritable and desperate to get home and so few paid me any attention. I watched as the other stall holders started to clear away, and soon after, my human and her colleague did the same. The signs got taken down and the game and entries were all packed safely away. My bed, the table, and all the other leaflets that were left were placed back in their bags and before long, the stall looked like we hadn't even been there. My human clipped my lead on, picked up her share of the equipment and with a large sigh, we all wearily made our way back across the showground to where the car was waiting.

The journey back took even longer than on the way there. We were all tired, and the going was made hard by the churned-up ground. Not only had people been walking about on it all day, but the bigger vehicles that could cope with the soft ground had made huge slippery divots that were hard to walk over. The buckets were also now heavy with money that had been donated throughout the day making the load more difficult than on the way in. I was just starting to think about what I could carry to help out, when my human lost her balance on a large clump of soil. Her leg slid from underneath her and pulled to the side at an awkward angle. She tried to steady herself, but in doing so let go of all the equipment she had been holding, which fell to the floor onto the muddy floor below: her hands landing either side, which at least stopped her from falling entirely. I felt my lead go slack as the loop landed by my side, but I knew now was not the time to go anywhere other than remain loyal to her side. As she righted herself, she looked down at her hands which were now covered in mud, and she let out a small chuckle. I felt the laughter was to hide her true feelings of annoyance and exhaustion, but nonetheless, it was nice to know she could still smile through it all. She set about cleaning her hands on the corner of her top, shrugging at her colleague as she did so; and then turned her attention to the equipment, which was still lying in a heap at her feet. She picked it all up, balancing it once again precariously in her arms: only this time, she had forgotten my lead which was still hanging by my side. She looked down and let out an exasperated sigh. She was just about to set her things down to make a space in her hand for my lead, when I realised this was my chance to help. I bent down and picked up the lead between my teeth. Realising my intention, she smiled and nodded,

"Good girl," she chuckled, and this time, I knew it wasn't to cover up other emotions.

Together, we made our way safely back to the car, me carrying my lead, and the two humans following on behind, laden to the brim with all their equipment. When we finally arrived and everything had been safely stowed away, we all collapsed into our respective seats. From the boot, I heard my human state, "never again," and while I was tired, I hoped she didn't mean it. I had enjoyed my day; I had seen so many new sights, met so many new people, and most of all, made more people aware of the work that we do. We had also raised money, which was evident by the buckets, and many people had said they would donate later via the internet.

I later found out she didn't mean it, and we have been to many other shows since. Luckily, the weather has been kinder to us, too, and we haven't needed to leave the car so far away, which, of course, made the days so much easier. I have also been recognised from one show to another and children have remembered some of the tricks I can do.

Now I can't quite say what I prefer doing: newspaper or magazine articles, filming for the news or social media or in person at events. All I know is it all makes me feel very special indeed. I can't help but feel famous when I see myself on TV or see my picture in an article, and it's truly overwhelming when people crowd around to watch me at a stall. However, I am also aware that no matter how much publicity I have taken part in, we are still struggling to raise the money for us to continue what we do. All I can do is continue to play my part and hope with all my heart that sometime soon the funding will be found for us to continue.

Yet another photoshoot

UNCERTAIN FUTURE

I am now five years old, and technically, in the prime of my life. I have been on my new food for a while now, and I feel better than ever. My human is in a good place, too; she is getting ready for her wedding next month and all is going well. Flo is happy too; the warmer weather has arrived, and the heat always seems to help her condition. I am not too fond of the heat, I seem to attract the sun's rays and get hotter far quicker than her. I like to rest in the shade, keeping my human safely in sight at all times. She seems to understand my dislike for the hotter parts of the day and will always ensure I am not out in it for too long. She often has a paddling pool filled up for me to cool off in after walks, or even better, finds somewhere where I can go for a swim. Sometimes, she even comes in and swims with me, which is the best feeling in the world.

Cuba is now rising eight and has come on leaps and bounds since I first met her. I sometimes sit and watch my human ride her, and I become entranced by the beauty of them together. They are forever learning new things, and while I have no idea what a lot of it means, I know that she makes my human very happy, and for me, that's all that really matters.

Some would say that life is pretty perfect at the moment, and for the most part, I would agree. However, each day that goes by, no matter how great things are, I know that there is a lingering question playing on my human's mind:

'What about the future?'

Now I know that no one knows what the future holds and sometimes it is pointless trying to second guess it; but sometimes, the future lies within your hands—and this is exactly how my human feels. With every day that goes by, a little bit of the funding we have goes with it, and the end of the scheme draws ever closer. She knows that if she sits back and does nothing then there is every chance that, before long, the term 'Brainy Dogs' will not exist. The dreams she had all those years ago, the work she has put in, the tricks I have learnt, and the publicity I have done will all amount to nothing. The potential clients will have to go elsewhere, and those that still turn to her for advice will be left without a phone number to ring.

Now I don't know if you agree with me, but I, for one, think this would be devastating—and not just for my human. When I think back to all the people I have met in my life, all the smiles I have seen, all the amazed carers and families when their loved ones respond to me in a way they haven't seen for so long, I just can't imagine not doing it anymore. I think back to the clients who now have their very own dogs, who, in turn, are changing their lives for the better; I wonder what they would have been doing if we hadn't have been here.

Despite this, my human continues to plan in the hope we can find funding from elsewhere. I heard her speaking about it the other day, and she spoke about all the plans she has, all of which included me, which I was pleased to hear.

From what I could gather, she wants to expand the scheme to a wider clientele; so no longer just helping those with a neurological condition, but many others, including people with mental health issues. When she mentioned this to a lady at the yard, who I later found out was a social worker, she became very excited. She explained how there is very little out there for people with mental health issues and that I could help a lot of people. I wasn't too sure what she meant by mental health issues; all I knew is my human would be with me and so I felt confident I could turn my paw to anything.

By widening the clientele base, my human is hoping to be able to reach more people through different organisations, too. She spoke about schools and other rehabilitation centres, along with other professionals, such as speech and language therapists and physiotherapists.

I mentioned to Flo about the plans, and when I mentioned the schools, her face lit up. She told me a story I had never heard before, in fact, I had no idea about it at all. Before I was around and before Flo suffered from her condition, she was taken to a school for children with special needs. It was before my human worked for Headway Suffolk and was one of the things that spurred her to continue pursuing her dream.

Flo told me how my human's sister-in-law worked as an assistant at the school, and she had told the staff all about her and the tricks she did. She also thought it would be a good opener for my human to set herself up in Animal Assisted Intervention. I always thought it would have been called Animal Assisted Therapy, but somewhere along the line, I found out my human couldn't be classed as a therapist. The only way she could have achieved this was to retrain down a particular route and then use dogs. I believe she considered it for a while, but with university bills still hanging over her head, it wasn't a financial possibility. However, she didn't let it dissuade her from her pursuing her dream, and thank god she didn't, otherwise, we wouldn't have been where we are today.

On the day they went to the school, they went into many classes. They were all small, with only a handful of children per room. Flo explained how she had never seen anything like it before—children running around making loud and unusual noises, others sat in their wheelchairs banging their fists on the tray in front of them. She told me how she had been worried when she first walked in, but as soon as they saw her, it was like a blanket of calm hit the room. Those that had been running walked over to their chairs. Those in wheelchairs stopped banging and stretched their hands out to where she was stood, and the screeching changed to noises of excitement and glee.

Once settled, she showed them all her tricks, which went down so well that she struggled to hear our human over the sound of laughing, cheering, and applause. She then went around them all one at a time, and some did tricks while others gave her a stroke. She remembered one of the children in particular; a young girl in a wheelchair. As she approached to say hello, the girl outstretched her arm to stroke her, but her movement was jerky and uncontrolled. Our human helped to steady her hand as she laid her fingers on Flo's soft coat. Our human helped her to stroke her arm along her back, but every now and again, her arm would jerk sideways and catch Flo in the side. As she spoke to me about the young girl, I could tell she became upset at the memory,

"At the time, I didn't mind, I knew the girl couldn't help it, and the smile on her face made it all worthwhile. But nowadays, I could never do anything like that for the pain would be too much."

Her eyes dropped to the floor, and she fell silent for a second. When ready, she continued on and told me all about the children in the other rooms. As she recalled her time spent in the school, I could tell she was proud of what she had achieved, and I felt excited that I, too, might get the opportunity to know what it felt like. However, I couldn't help but feel her sadness as she spoke, and I knew now was not the time to express my excitement. When I asked her why I had not heard about this before, she merely replied

"Because this was the one thing I had that you have not. I have watched you do everything that I used to be able to do, and then more. My time spent in that school was something only I have experienced, and I enjoyed keeping those memories to myself."

With that, she turned away and walked over to her bed, and I knew that was the end of the conversation.

After listening to Flo, I knew that my human was right in wanting to also start going into schools. I thought about the tricks I could do that they might enjoy most and also the activities that might help them. My mind went into overdrive, and I realised that lots of what I do could be altered to be beneficial to them. Again, I felt myself feeling excited about the prospect of going forward; but I was quickly brought back to earth when I remembered we may not even be able to continue.

In addition to schools, my human also wants to work alongside other therapists to aid people's rehabilitation from trauma. I heard her talking about it one day to Janice, and she explained how she thought it would work better this way than her specialising in one particular area. Her plan would be for her and me to work alongside the therapists to plan specific activities to the individual based upon the care plan built by the therapist.

To start with, I was confused about how this would work, I mean, I could understand how people thought the tricks I do are fun; but I wasn't sure how it could help a physiotherapist, for example. However, shortly after the conversation, a gentleman came in who I hadn't seen before. He walked with the use of a stick, but it was clear he had a left-sided weakness. He struggled to pick his left leg up as he walked; instead, he moved it out to the side and around in front of him. His left arm was contracted to his chest, but it appeared he did have some movement in it. He sat down, and my human had a quick talk with him and then called me over. She started off by showing him what tricks I can do and then he had a turn. It started off very similar to what I did on my visits, however, this time, she concentrated on using his weak side to give the commands. This made it harder for me to understand what he wanted, but once again, my human was there to back up the command when I was a little confused. After this, we did the activity where my human placed out two toys on opposite sides. The gentleman had to choose which toy he wanted me to go to first; if it was to the right, he used his stronger arm, and his weaker arm to the left. We played this a few times, and it took all my concentration to work out which toy I was to collect first. However, when we finished, he turned to my human and said,

"This is just like physio!!"

It was at that exact moment that I realised how easily I could work alongside therapists: we had just basically done it by ourselves. I started to picture just how much we could do with a therapist helping us to specialise the activities for everyone, and I became very excited, I even felt my tail wag at the mere thought of it.

After this, the gentleman came back, and we spent time doing many different activities. Some days, we went for a walk; each time, the gentleman trying to walk a bit further. He told my human he preferred walking with me as it gave him a purpose, and he enjoyed the conversation as it made the walk seem easier.

Other days, he would sit and groom me, again concentrating on using his weaker side. He also used this opportunity to improve the time he could stand for. Again, he told my human he found it much easier when he was working with me as he never became bored.

When I watched my human with the clients, it was clear how much passion she had for her job. When she spoke to them in between activities, she had a look on her face that I never saw at any other time. When they managed to do something that they hadn't managed before, it was clear that she, too, felt their accomplishments within herself. It was times like this that I knew she did her job more for the passion she felt, rather than to make a living; and I felt honoured that I could do my bit alongside her.

As well as expanding to schools and working alongside therapists, I know that my human has even grander plans for the scheme. The biggest idea she has would be to have her very own centre where she could train dogs and have sessions for rehab. This means that she could still go out into the community and do her visits but would also enable people to come and have group sessions within the centre.

I only came to find out about this idea when I stumbled across a piece of paper, which had it all written down. We had been out for the day on visits and so my human returned me home to rest before she went back up to the yard to see Cuba. I waited for her to leave and then settled myself on the sofa beside Flo. I must have fallen straight to sleep, for the next thing I knew, I was waking from a dream. I must have been animated in my dream as I had knocked some papers from the coffee table next to me on to the floor. I got down to see what had been knocked off, and I couldn't help but notice the detailed plan of a centre on the largest piece of paper.

From what I could gather, the centre was to include both indoor and outdoor areas. Outside there was to be kennels so the dogs could be trained individually without distracting each other. There were then different areas for different activities; such as agility, off lead exercise/training, and temptation alley. Around the perimeter was a path mapped out where the dogs could be walked, this could either be for exercise or for clients to improve their walking. Inside there was an office, a toilet, a small kitchen area for making hot drinks, and a couple of rooms. One of the rooms was marked out for client sessions and one was set out to be for training of dogs.

Next to the drawing, my human had written down some key points of what the centre would be used for. These included training of dogs for clients and the training of dogs for visits and client sessions. In my head, I started to picture what the centre could look like, and before long, my imagination had taken over. I pictured dogs in kennels, waiting to be trained to make a difference to their new human's life. I pictured others being trained in the outside pens, either to run past the treats back to their handler, ignoring the toys and treats on the floor, or having a go at the agility to improve their listening skills to the handler. I pictured another dog working on its recall alongside its new owner in the large outside area, forming a bond together that would last a lifetime. Inside, I saw myself working with a group of clients, helping them to work on different skills. I imagined what new activities my human would come up with given the opportunity within the new centre. Maybe she would purchase new equipment, think of new games for us to play, and above all, help the clients.

As I lay there thinking of the centre, I couldn't help but see the potential it would bring to my human and the ways in which she could help people. I knew that the dream of hers was big, and not only would it need funding—but it would need big funding. It would also need more people rather than just her to be able to make it work. I was just starting to wonder who these people might be when I noticed a couple of points written in smaller writing on the plan. The first one said 'Collaboration/partnership?', and beside this was a list of other organisations. It became clear to me that maybe this wasn't such a pipe dream of my human's, maybe this was something she was seriously considering. At this moment, I happened to look up and I noticed a saying my human had purchased and hung above the door in the living room. It read:

'Wish it, Dream it, Do it.'

I began to realise the importance of the words; they weren't just there for decoration, but instead, they were there to keep motivating my human to believe in herself and chase her dreams. She had also written above the plan the words "Where there's a will….there's a way." I had heard her say this saying many times, and it was something she had always stuck to. There wasn't one time when I had known my human to give up. In fact, she was quite often ridiculed for her stubbornness, but it was times like this that I realised it was her attitude and her refusal to give up that had brought her this far. As I laid there, I realised that if it was at all possible, then my human would make it happen: and I couldn't help but feel proud that she belonged to me.

Then I read the other words which were written in smaller writing, and I felt my heart skip a beat, they read 'New dog needed'. Instantly, I panicked; had I not done a good enough job all these years? Did my human feel the need to replace me? Would she rehome me? Would I go to Lily?

All these questions were flying around my head when I heard the front door open, and my human returned from the yard. She removed her boots and made her way into the lounge where I was laid with the plan still firmly underneath my paws. She walked over, carefully removed the plan, and returned it to the coffee table, giving it a quick look over as she did. She then looked back at me and gave me a sly smile,

"What do you reckon Hope? Reckon we could make it work?"

She had said 'we', implying that I would still be involved, but I couldn't shake the words 'new dog' from my brain, and for the first time, I really worried about the future.

It wasn't until a couple of days later when she produced the plan to Janice that I was finally able to settle. She went through all the ideas and dreams she had about the centre, and how great it would be if ever it could be made a success. As she spoke, I listened intently, waiting for her to mention my name or talk about my replacement: I didn't have to wait long:

"Obviously, with the added workload, I wouldn't be able to just use Hope, I would need another dog, if not two. Although, I'm not sure I would want another lab—I couldn't cope with more hairs around the place!"

With that, she started chuckling and pointed to the loose hairs that I had dislodged after a good scratch. I knew my moulting hairs bugged her as she was forever moaning at home about the number of times she needed to sweep up. I had tried many times to stop it, but no matter what I did, I always left a small trail of hair where ever I went.

However, the good news was—I wasn't being replaced! I can't tell you how happy and relieved I was when I heard the words come out of her mouth. After this, my human carried on talking about the plans, but I couldn't help but let my mind wander to what new dog my human might get. I thought of all the dogs that had been on the scheme; of all the different breeds and crossbreeds. I knew some were easier to teach than others, and I knew from my own training that the new dog would have to enjoy learning like I had done. I knew that it would need to have high retrieval instincts as most of the games we played involved fetching something. It would also need to enjoy being busy and also enjoy being outside, as when not at work, I spent a lot of time at the yard. I thought of many breeds which may be suitable, but I also knew it would depend on the dog itself. I found myself looking forward to having a new dog around the place, and I thought of all the ways I could pass on my knowledge so it found it easier to learn what was needed. However, it wasn't long until my thoughts turned to Flo and how she would feel. I worried that she might feel even more pushed out, and the new dog might even stop her coming the few visits she can manage. I decided it was best not to say anything, I didn't want to worry her unnecessarily, and at the moment, it was all just talk, anyway.

So as I lay here now, I think back to everything I have been through in my five years.

I think of the farmer, my mother, and my siblings. I wonder what they are up to, if any are doing something similar to me. I wonder if my mother rekindled her bond with the farmer and if she is happy.

I think of the puppy I once was; of the long ears and stumpy legs. I think of the humans that called me useless and of those that laughed at me for how I looked. But mostly, I wonder if my mother knew me now, would she be proud?

I think of Tilly, of the good times we had and of all the things she taught me. I wonder if I would be where I am today if it hadn't been for her guidance from the start. I wonder if she is watching down on me, sat with my human's grandparents and the man from the care home. I wonder if they are proud of my human, and if they are helping in some way for her to achieve her goals.

I think of the all the dogs I have worked with in the past and if they are still helping their humans in a way no one else could. I think of Pippa and hope she is happy, that she never lost her fun approach to life and is continuing to help Tony find his confidence and independence.

I think of all those in the care homes that I have visited. I remember the smiles and laughter we shared together and of all those achievements they made with me and my human at their side.

I think of all the walks I have been on with my human; the places I have discovered and the adventures we have had together. I think of Brad and Chief and how my human's life has changed since they joined our family. I think of my human and the ups and downs she has endured with friends. I think of Cuba and all the achievements my human has made with her, and lastly, I think of Flo; of how she has sat back and watched me take over her life through no fault of her own. I think back to the depressed dog I first met when I arrived as a puppy. I think of how our friendship has grown and how now I would be lost without her.

As I think about the past, I can't help but worry that things will change. However, at the same time, I am excited that it might change for the better. The mixed emotions I feel now are hard to put into words. I hope with all my heart, that no matter what happens with my human's job, it won't stop her being my human. I hope that she can continue to follow her dreams, and that I will be the one walking proudly by her side.

However, I cannot predict the future, and so for now, I will carry on as I have been for the last five years. I will continue to be loyal to those I love and give my heart and soul to the work that I do. And I know, no matter what the future holds, that I can hold my head up high: for I have made a difference. I, the dog that was no good for anything, am helping people; and all I can do is pray that my job never has to end.

EVERYBODY NEEDS HOPE

If you would like to contact my human or her colleagues then I have put the contact details below.

Maybe you could kindly make a donation or they may be able to help you.

HEADWAY SUFFOLK
GROUND FLOOR
EPSILON HOUSE
WEST ROAD
RANSOMES EUROPARK
IPSWICH
IP3 9FJ

brainydogs@hotmail.co.uk

01473 712225

Printed in Poland
by Amazon Fulfillment
Poland Sp. z o.o., Wrocław